THOMAS
MERTON

"I cannot imagine anyone else doing the book so beautifully"
JOHN HOWARD GRIFFIN

"This should be a perennial reference book and general explanation of Merton in its highly condensed and readable form. There is the kind of frankness Merton would have liked and not a false note anywhere. . . . I am glad finally that there is a book I can wholeheartedly recommend as true to Merton. . . . I am spellbound by the spectacular research [the authors] managed to cram into these pages. The explanations are beautiful and right in tone—not a touch of condescension or pietism. Tom must have sat next to [their] reading chair and typewriters."

JOHN HOWARD GRIFFIN

"This is an absorbing biography of the mystic who founded his tenets not only on the great saints of Roman Catholicism but on the teachings of Zen, Aldous Huxley and Bob Dylan. Young readers should welcome enthusiastically the Süssmans' revelations of the man who championed the Civil Rights Movement, protests against the war in Vietnam and other causes from behind the walls of a monastery."

Publishers Weekly

"The first full-length biography of Merton for any age group. . . . Not every reader will be temperamentally suited to the Süssmans' approach, but it does crack open a door of sorts to Merton's own writing and, on the strength of that alone, should make a place for itself."

Kirkus Reviews

"What a lovely book . . . I enjoyed it very much, especially the letter to Huxley re drugs, which I'd never seen before, and the encounter with Suzuki."

ANNE FREEMANTLE

". . . follows the life of Thomas Merton, twentieth-century mystic, Trappist monk, hermit and peace activist, from his bohemian childhood to his tragic death in Bangkok in 1968 . . ."

The Booklist

". . . a worthy addition to the list of writings on Merton. The Süssmans have written a very popular, interpretative, even dramatic biography of the priest who became the hero of yesterday's intellectuals. The book is highly recommended, especially for Parish libraries."

The Priest

". . . fills a large lacuna in Mertoniana . . ."

Cistercian Studies

"I devoured the book in one sitting. It is a gem. You have caught him and conveyed simply and truly the towering earthy human he was . . ."

REV. WILLIAM McNAMARA, O.C.D.

"Mr. and Mrs. Süssman have painted a glowing portrait of a man whom they obviously admire as scholar and saint; yet they do not lose sight of his essential humanity and its inherent frailties."

The Saginaw News

THOMAS MERTON

CORNELIA & IRVING SUSSMAN

REVISED EDITION

IMAGE BOOKS
A DIVISION OF DOUBLEDAY & COMPANY, INC.
GARDEN CITY, NEW YORK
1980

Image Book edition published September 1980 by special arrangement with
Macmillan Publishing Co., Inc.

Grateful acknowledgment is made to the following for permission to quote from
copyrighted material: Excerpt on page 37 from *My Argument With the Gestapo:
A Macaronic Journal* by Thomas Merton, copyright © 1968 by Thomas Merton,
copyright © 1969 by The Abbey of Gethsemani, Inc., reprinted by permission of
Doubleday & Company, Inc.; excerpts on pages 13 and 19 from *Mystics and Zen
Masters* by Thomas Merton, copyright © 1961, 1962, 1964, 1965, 1966, 1967 by
The Abbey of Gethsemani, Inc., reprinted by permission of Farrar, Straus &
Giroux, Inc.; excerpt on page 98 from *The Seven Storey Mountain* by Thomas
Merton, copyright © 1948 by Harcourt Brace Jovanovich, Inc., reprinted by
permission of the publisher; excerpts on pages 111 and 122 from *The Sign of
Jonas* by Thomas Merton, copyright © 1953 by The Abbey of Our Lady of
Gethsemani, reprinted by permission of Harcourt Brace Jovanovich, Inc.;
excerpt on page 27 from *Collected Poems* (In One Volume) by Alfred Noyes,
copyright © 1906, renewed 1934 by Alfred Noyes, reprinted by permission of
J. B. Lippincott Company; excerpt on page 136 from *The Asian Journal of
Thomas Merton*, copyright © 1973 by The Trustees of the Thomas Merton
Literary Property Trust, reprinted by permission of New Directions Publishing
Corporation; excerpts on pages 70 and 85 from *Cables to the Ace* by Thomas
Merton, copyright © 1968 by The Abbey of Gethsemani, Inc., reprinted by
permission of New Directions Publishing Corporation; excerpts on pages 49 and
57 from *The Geography of Lograire* by Thomas Merton, copyright © 1968–69
by The Merton Legacy Trust, reprinted by permission of New Directions
Publishing Corporation.

LIBRARY OF CONGRESS CATALOGING IN PUBLICATION DATA
Süssman, Cornelia Silver.
Thomas Merton.
Bibliography.
Includes index.
SUMMARY: A biography of the Trappist monk and Zen
mystic who gained fame as a writer, social critic, and
radical peace activist.
1. Merton, Thomas, 1915–1968—Juvenile literature.
[1. Merton, Thomas, 1915–1968. 2. Authors, American]
I. Süssman, Irving, joint author.
BX4705.M542S9   271'.125'024 [B]   [92]
Library of Congress Catalog Card Number: 80-924
ISBN 0-385-17172-2

I am about to make my home
In the bell's summit
Set my mind a thousand feet high
On the ace of songs. . . .

I am about to build my nest
In the misdirected and unpaid express
As I walk away from this poem

Hiding the ace of freedoms

Thomas Merton
Cables to the Ace

CONTENTS

ACKNOWLEDGMENTS

The authors gratefully acknowledge the generous benefits of the thoughts, commentaries, and memories of numerous friends of Thomas Merton, and the assistance the following sources afforded them in checking the authenticity and accuracy of factual biographical material. However, we, the authors, are alone responsible for the expression of ideas and the viewpoint of this biography.

We express our thanks to David Reuther; to the staff of the Thomas Merton Collection at Bellarmine College; to the Trustees of the Merton Legacy Trust; and, most particularly, to John Howard Griffin. We express our appreciation to the many others who shared impressions and memories of Thomas Merton with us, in conversations, letters, on tapes, and via other communications. Among them: Fr. William McNamara, OCD, of The Spiritual Life Institute of America and Canada; J. Stanley Murphy, CSB, of Assumption University, and Director of the Christian Culture Series; Father August Thompson; Mother Myriam Dardenne of Our Lady of the Redwoods Abbey, Whitethorne, California; Catherine Doherty; James Forest; Naomi Burton; Laura Huxley; John and Barbara Beecher.

The authors would like, especially, to thank Brother Patrick Hart, OCSO, Abbey of Gethsemani, Kentucky, for reading and suggesting improvements in the manuscript of this book.

1

The Mind is like a clear mirror standing.
Take care to wipe it all the time. . . .

He looked like a boy standing at the rail, watching the mountains of water bear down on the ship; he looked like a slender, fair, shy English boy. But he was not a boy, he was only partly a boy. Already he had experienced much that a man must experience, or thinks he must.

Young Tom Merton was not quite twenty on this crossing of the Atlantic Ocean from England to the United States, in late November of 1934. It was a stormy crossing, and the turbulent seas echoed the turbulence of his mind. He was leaving the Europe of his childhood with its ceaseless journeyings here and there, and he was leaving the England of his adolescence with its depths of unhappiness. He was leaving England forever.

He had been studying at Clare College, in England; but Cambridge soured after one year of study there. It had gone very fast, that freshman year. "I was breaking my neck trying to get everything out of life that you think you can get out of it when you are eighteen. . . ."

Now, on board the ship to the United States, he saw all

the times he had crossed this Atlantic Ocean, saw them coming in on wave after wave.

The first crossing took place when he was just one year old —all he knew of the journey was what he'd heard his parents say, mostly that the boat had a gun mounted on its foredeck to protect them from the German U-boats. His mother was an American, his father was from New Zealand. They were artists who had met in Paris. After they were married they kept searching for inexpensive places where poor young artists could afford to live.

That was how they happened to come to Prades, a small French town near the border of Spain. They stayed barely long enough for Tom to be born and then left. He was born on January 31, 1915, under the sign of Aquarius.

Even at the moment of his birth, the cannons of World War I were booming. "Not many hundreds of miles away from the house where I was born, they were picking up the men who rotted in the rainy ditches among the dead horses . . . in a forest of trees without branches along the river Marne."

Tom's mother was a pacifist and she was afraid his father would join up. Also, Tom's maternal grandparents were worried about the family being in a land at war. So the Mertons went to America.

Hanging onto the rail, listening to the groans of stanchion and bulkhead while the ship reeled and soared up to the wet sky and then swept down into the dark troughs, Tom let his memory drift. He had a good memory. Vividly he recalled things that had happened in earliest childhood; the ten years growing up in America were clear. It was after that things had begun to get more complicated.

His mother died of cancer of the stomach when he was six, and all those months she was in the hospital he never went to see her. He couldn't, because his mother believed children should not have to learn about sadness so early. Sickness and death were to be kept from them, so Tom and his three-year-old brother, John Paul, were "protected."

During his mother's illness he and his brother lived with

their grandparents. Tom understood little about his mother's illness; he was carefree. His grandparents had two dogs and several cats for him to play with, and he could run in the woods nearby. But one day his father gave him a note to read. He was surprised because it was for him personally, in his mother's handwriting. She had never written to him before. In the letter she told him she was about to die and would never see him again. Fiercely, he ran away, took the note out under the maple tree in the yard. There, by himself, he worked over it until he knew it by heart and understood what it really meant. A tremendous weight of sadness and depression settled on him.

He shook himself, to shake off the reverie the surging waves had brought on. But he could not so easily shake off the thoughts of a young man who is growing a mustache and knows that adulthood can't be put off much longer. Four years earlier, when he was sixteen, he'd made this same sea voyage, full of high spirits and a yen for romance. He had a brand-new suit and soon found the prettiest girl aboard ship to fall for; she was twice sixteen but he didn't know that, and wouldn't have cared. Age was of the least importance.

He talked to her about all his ideas—wanting to be a famous writer, his dreams, hopes, ambitions. She talked a lot, too, about movie stars and a prince she met in a famous night club who had stared at her intently. On the last night, as the ship approached New York harbor, a great ball was in progress. Music filled the air and everybody was dancing except Tom, who had never learned to dance. For a few minutes he was able to corner her and tell her, in a rush of words, how much he loved her and that he would love her forever. She smiled sweetly, pleased, and said it could never be, and she had to rush because her dance program was full. He felt gruesomely silly.

All his dreams—the desire to be a sailor, a rover of strange lands, a writer of novels and adventurous tales—were empty. His dreams about experiencing fantastic pleasures and delights were crazy. He had always been told to search for a way of life that would bring him success and happiness, but what he had found so far was meaningless! Everything he'd reached for had turned to ashes.

That's how everything was, absurd. Dust and ashes in his hands. He had been to Soviet Russian movies, and had read books about Soviet Russia. It seemed the only place where true art could find a refuge in a world of bourgeois capitalist materialism. Cambridge had left him profoundly disillusioned. The only thing he got out of Cambridge was learning about Dante, all the rest was pollution.

At this moment, Tom looked up to see a hardy seafaring man on deck—an old gentleman. He paused and said to Tom, enigmatically: "When the storm's outside 'tis wise to go inside." Then he winked, tapped the side of his head, and moved along.

Tom laughed. He looked around the wide decks and noted the few passengers who had ventured forth. Then he turned back to the sea, the unpitying sea.

"When the storm's outside, go inside." Strange lands had always called to him, fascinated him; but the strange land inside himself was something else again. Outer space was fascinating—he didn't really care about inner space. It wasn't an impressive landscape, he decided.

"Tom," he muttered, "you're an unpleasant sort of person, very." He could see himself as though looking in a mirror, and he said: "I am vain, self-centered, dissolute, weak, irresolute, undisciplined, sensual, obscene, and proud." He paused for breath, then went on: "I'm a mess."

Then, as suddenly as it had come, his religious fervor vanished. But something had happened in that inner world of himself. There had been an earth movement. He felt a deep disgust with himself. There had to be something more to life. Life had to have a deeper meaning than those clichés and slogans he heard all around him about making a success, about being patriotic, about finding happiness with Greta Garbo in a cottage small by a waterfall, about being at the top of organizations, politics, power.

He remembered a strange experience he'd had nearly two years ago. It was right after his eighteenth birthday. He'd gone up to Cambridge for the scholarship exams and was successful, so his guardian gave him the money for a trip to

Italy. One night in Rome, he had the eerie experience of meeting his dead father. He was in his room. His father, who had been dead for a year, appeared to him.

For the first time in his life Tom really prayed. He prayed for himself, not just with his lips but with the roots of his being. The next morning he climbed the deserted Aventine in the spring sun and went into the Dominicans' Church, Santa Sabina, with the idea of kneeling down and praying. He had been in many churches, ruined chapels, and Gothic cathedrals for artistic or historical reasons, but he had never deliberately walked into a church to pray. It was a new experience, and an embarrassing one. He was sure an old Italian woman praying before one of the statues was examining him with suspicious eyes and would report him to the authorities any minute. But he managed to get down on his knees for a few seconds to say a prayer.

For a few months after that he was fascinated by religion and would hide in corners, reading the Bible surreptitiously for fear someone would catch him at it and make fun of him. Then, as suddenly as it had come, his religious fervor vanished.

The ten-day liner from England to New York was nearing its goal. They passed Nantucket Light and the long, low, yellow shoreline of Long Island appeared. There was New York harbor with its glittering lights, the great, debonair city.

As Tom walked down the gangplank, a feeling of excitement filled his heart, a great feeling of confidence overwhelmed him. It came so strongly after his intense depression that he felt carried away. He felt like the Count of Monte Cristo and let out a yell: "New York, you are mine! I love you!"

He was glad. Like many sensitive persons, young or old, Tom felt that despite his confusion, his lack of beliefs, the absurdity of his moments of clarity—despite all this, life was good.

Like Pierre in Tolstoy's *War and Peace*, Tom realized that life is the day-to-day living of it, and though Pierre was but a character in a book, he was Tom's close friend, a friend to heed. To live one day at a time was the only way to live life to the full, and to learn from his past what his future could be.

"New York, you are mine! I love you!" Tom repeated as he came down the gangplank to the dock.

But as it turned out, things were not that simple. He had more to cross than the Atlantic Ocean. He was out of Europe, but Europe was still in him, and the prospect of going to a new school, in a new world, carried along with it all the old schools of the old world.

2

We make doors and windows for a room
But it is these empty spaces that make the room livable. . . .

He was home again. His grandparents' house in Douglaston, Long Island, was where his parents had brought him at age one. It was the house he and John Paul had lived in when his mother was dying in the hospital. The maple tree still stood in the back yard, the one under which he had sat and read the only letter his mother ever wrote him. And his room was waiting, with its glass-enclosed bookcases which he began to fill with his own books—books on psychoanalysis, a Vulgate Bible he'd bought in Rome, Communist pamphlets, and the *Enneads* of Plotinus—a huge volume he dragged home on the subway and the Long Island railroad.

He was home. Yet he really had no home, or maybe he had too many homes. Tom had lived in more places by this time than most people do in a lifetime. If you asked him: "What's your nationality?" he would think a minute and reply: "I have lived in too many countries to have a nationality." Nationality was a state of mind, he decided—and, if that was so, he was French in mentality more than American.

After his mother's death, Tom had gone to Cape Cod with his father for a summer. That was the summer he got mumps and his father read him poems by John Masefield. Then winter came and Tom was returned to his grandparents' house. His father soon returned and took him away again, this time to Bermuda. His father would paint; sometimes he'd stay away for a few days, going places with other artists. Tom went to the local school, but not always—he didn't go on days when they had multiplication and division.

Tom's father had lost the ability to paint after the death of his wife, he was so emptied out from grief. But now the gift had been given back. Critics in London and in other art centers said Owen Merton was one of the master watercolorists. They spoke of his "pure use of space."

Now his father was painting more pictures, and art galleries were having more exhibitions of his paintings. It became harder for him to take Tom along on his travels, so he brought him back to the house in Douglaston once again and off he went. Tom got letters from strange and exotic lands—even Africa. One time a package came containing a small burnoose that Tom could wear.

Then a letter came saying that Owen Merton was dying. Tom's grandmother told him the news. Unbearably affected, Tom grieved in solitude, fearing he would never see his father again. For days his father lay in delirium, expected to die at any moment. Then the crisis passed. He regained consciousness and recovered so completely that he finished his pictures and held a successful exhibition in London. As soon as the exhibit was over, Owen Merton returned to see Tom and John Paul—the sons he had thought he would never see again.

Tom, age ten, hadn't seen his father for two years. He looked strange, he had a beard! Tom didn't like it. The first thing he said was, "Are you going to shave it off now or later?" His father said, "I'm not going to shave it off at all."

The illness had made Owen Merton determined not to be separated ever again from his boys, at least not while they were growing up. He didn't want to leave them in the care of others. He resolved to find a place in France for all of them. There he could be at the center of the artistic and literary world so necessary to an artist. At the same time he could make a home for his sons to grow up under his own care. He decided to take only Tom with him this trip, as John Paul was too young.

At first Tom had not wanted to leave his friends, but as the time drew near he became more enthusiastic about going away with his father. Now his father talked to him not as a child but as an adult. He pointed out that there was more to life than the ambitions for making money and business success which motivated most Americans in the twenties. Things were different in France.

France in the 1920s was the artistic, literary, and spiritual center of the world—James Joyce, Ernest Hemingway, F. Scott Fitzgerald, Gertrude Stein, Picasso and Rouault, Henri Bergson, and Stravinsky lived there.

On a rainy September evening in 1925 they arrived in Calais. "At the age of ten," said Merton later, "I already knew I was going to like France."

They immediately boarded a train and rode through the night until they came to a dark, silent town. It was Montauban on the border of Languedoc. The air was lovely at Montauban and the low tile-roofed houses were attractive. But the streets had a deathlike quality. When they walked to the hotel, the woman in black behind the desk was rude.

They decided not to stay long in Montauban. About ten or fifteen miles north, they discovered St. Antonin, an ancient town whose history dated from Roman days. To walk its streets was to be in the Middle Ages. At the center of town, the church stood on the ruins of the ancient shrine of St. Antonin; its bells rang out the Angelus each noon and evening.

There Tom's father rented an apartment and planned to build a house of his own as soon as possible. Presently he bought a fine piece of land. Ten-year-old Tom was placed in the local elementary school. Tom was miserably embarrassed at first because he was older than the others. But there was no way around it—he had to take his place among the smallest children and start learning French.

In spite of the embarrassment of having to be in the same class with the smallest children, Tom discovered he was happy. Southern France was having a mad love affair with the game of Rugby football, and since Tom's father was an Englishman, the town immediately made him president of the local Rugby club. They would tear all around the countryside on wild rides with the Rugby team.

By summer, Tom had learned all the French a boy of eleven could be expected to know. Next fall he would enter the Lycée Ingres, but first there was summer vacation. His maternal grandparents, whom he called Pop and Bonnemaman, arrived with John Paul on a grand European tour. Tom and his father joined them in Paris.

The minute they entered the Hotel Continental where Pop and Bonnemaman were staying, they knew it was a bad show. The hotel was expensive beyond Pop's means and he'd bought all kinds of useless things wherever they went, so that the hotel room was crammed to the doors. Soon they were all at their nerves' ends and fighting over silly things.

Next stop on the tour was Switzerland. In the train climbing the Jungfrau, Tom argued with his grandfather about which peaks were higher. His grandfather angrily said other peaks appeared much higher than the Jungfrau. Tom kept arguing with him that the Jungfrau only looked lower because of the perspective.

By the time they were back at their hotel, Tom burst into nervous tears in the dining room. Then he and his father and John Paul walked outside into a bright snowfield without dark glasses and got painful headaches. To put the finishing touches on their misery, John Paul fell fully dressed into a pond in front of one of the really smart hotels, and came walking into the lobby—where people stood or sat, elegant and amused—dripping water, green weeds, and with little fishes in his hair. Tom vowed never to go sightseeing with anybody ever again.

Once back in France, Tom hid from them all. He read *Tarzan of the Apes* and had finished the whole book by the time everyone returned from seeing the Palace of the Popes. They told him he'd missed a lot, but he felt happy—reading by himself.

As with all summer vacations, there was one beautiful day. On Bastille Day, July 14, they came to the town of Dijon, on the Côte d'Or—the shore of gold.

Their father carried the suitcase up to their room at the Hotel Rocamadour and began to unpack, while John Paul and Tom stood and watched him. The smell of his tobacco, his artist's paints, pervaded everything—it was like a good "family" smell. The three Mertons.

Then father and sons went forth to watch the parade in the big square. The horsemen were dressed in finery, their shining plumed helmets shimmering in the late light of evening. The horses' hoofs made a soft clopping sound over the cobblestones. Strings of colored bulbs cast a serene light on the streets. Years later, Merton was to write, "Dijon, you sing to me in the nights of summer like the fifes of my ten years' age, and your dusk is all entranced with lights, like strings of beads!"

Dreamily, the boys watched the horses toss their manes. The bugles sounded. The dark, green trees danced stately in the summer wind. Presently they drifted along to a small music store and stood looking at the upright pianos inside. The window was full of ocarinas, harmonicas, flageolets, little flutes, and there was a violin in an open case. The smell of new sheet music wafted out and called them in, so in they went. Tom wandered around, vaguely aware his little brother was back there among the pianos. Suddenly someone began to play the piano. It was his father. There he was, seated at one of the upright keyboards. He had put his pipe down on the end of the keyboard and was playing and singing in a loud bouncy voice:

"Chicago, Chicago . . ." And as soon as he finished that, he went into: "Tea for two and two for tea . . ." and he topped them all off with a vehement rendering: "I won't be happy, till I make you happy to-o-o. . . ." He did make them happy, and happy they walked back to the Hotel Rocamadour.

The town of Montauban boasted of many things, not the least of which was the school for *les enfants*, the Lycée Ingres. The French lycées were schools for students worthy of top-rated secondary education. The state appointed the professors and they had to be highly trained, for they taught academic courses of strict quality; courses approved by the state.

This was what Tom's father was told, and it was, ideally, the way the lycées were run. What Tom's father was not told (it wasn't broadly advertised) was that qualified professors often were not available. Most scholars did not look forward to teaching the young ruffians who entered their classes. They preferred some other outlet for their knowledge—working on encyclopedias, for example, was less nerve-racking. As a result many lesser trained teachers, called teachers' aides, *chargés de cours*, were the ones who taught the classes. They were not usually inspired or inspiring, and their knowledge was often even more inadequate than their teaching.

For Tom Merton, the years at Lycée Ingres were as if spent in a horror chamber. The first day, out in the big graveled schoolyard, he was surrounded by a group of large boys whose dark, glittering eyes seemed to flash contempt for his pale, blue-eyed, round English face. Like chickens who will peck to death the wild duckling unlucky enough to enter their domain, the boys wished to destroy the outsider. They shouted at him, loud taunting words, obscenities, and screamed unanswerable questions. Tom didn't respond. This was enraging. That the new boy should stand up to their curses and threats appeared altogether too courageous. They knocked him down on the gravel, kicked him, fell on him, and nearly twisted his ears off. They rubbed his knees in the sharp gravel until blood flowed. He didn't cry out. His silence was maddening; yet it wasn't courage or pride that kept Tom silent. The truth was that the minute he looked into those many hostile eyes, he forgot every word of French he knew. He couldn't answer.

Bruised, battered, bleeding, ears ringing from blows and also from obscenities, he somehow managed to get to his feet —day after day, for this went on and on.

He pleaded with his father to get him out of that awful school. But there was no way his father could change schools without sending Tom even farther away. And he'd have to live at whichever lycée he attended, as room and board were compulsory in Merton's time.

At first Tom used to go home nearly every Sunday, taking the early morning train from Montauban to St. Antonin. And his father also tried to ease things for Tom by taking him to spend the Christmas holidays with a kind, warm-hearted, devout peasant family, M. and Mme. Privat.

That summer, seeing how thin Tom was from the many fevers he had gone through during the winter at the lycée, his father sent Tom to live with the Privats. They built him up by feeding him butter and milk and good nourishing food.

As it happened, the house that Tom's father had dreamed of building for himself and his sons never worked out. He traveled too much. Art exhibits made it necessary to be at the galleries where his paintings were being shown. And he had many friends in the world of arts and letters who invited him to visit. There he could meet important critics and patrons of the arts. He was always having to go off to Paris, or to Marseille, or to Cette (a Mediterranean port), or back to England for yet another exhibition. Tom had to resign himself to the school, so he did. He got accustomed to life at the Lycée Ingres.

The children Tom had known at St. Antonin and in other schools had been rough and mischievous at times, but never vicious. There seemed true demonic possession among the boys at the lycée, with all the characteristics of sadistic cruelty, filth, obscenity, envy, and hatred of goodness. As Merton remarked years later: "Contact with that wolf-pack felt very patently like contact with the mystical body of the devil."

At last, the big bullies began to leave him alone. He found a group of peaceful children, and soon Tom was one of their crowd. Presently, they were all furiously writing novels. On the walks the boys had to take, two by two into the countryside in a long line, Tom's group would walk in a superior way —caps on the backs of heads, hands in pockets—like great intellectuals.

Three years in the prison of the lycée. He had learned much there, he later decided. He had found a place to go where no one could follow—through books. He had also learned about people, the schoolboys, the teachers, the fierce little *censeur* (proctor) of the lycée with his thin, wispy mustache. He had learned about those possessed by devils and those possessed by angels. He would never forget the days and nights in the infirmary. The silence of dark nights suddenly pierced by the high-pitched, forlorn whistle of the train or the clanging of the church bell. The silence again. Then the slippered shuffle of the night watchman along the hall.

He never forgot the lessons learned from being a prisoner for three years at the Lycée Ingres. All his life he would have an affinity for the outsider.

One bright May morning, his father unexpectedly came to the lycée and Tom was called down to the main room to meet him. He told Tom to go get his things, they were leaving for England. Tom felt like a person who has just had chains struck from his hands. The prison gates had burst open.

In the cab with his father, he heard the horse's hoofs clopping: "Liberty! Liberty! Liberty!" all the way to the station. Then they were racing through Picardy on the Nord railway, and then they were on the channel steamer. Ahead lay Folkestone cliffs and Ealing.

3

There is a barrel-organ carolling across a golden street
In the City as the sun sinks low. . . .

London is a city of poetic golden streets. Shafts of light pour
through the sea mists and the fog as the sun sinks low. At
first sight all the centuries of historic London rise up, immortal. Chaucer and Shakespeare, Blake and Dickens walked
these streets.

For Tom, the best thing about Ealing was that it was just
nine miles from London on the wonderful double-deck bus
his Aunt Maud took him on, first thing. Ealing was also the
house at 18 Carlton Road where Aunt Maud and Uncle Ben
lived in Victorian durability. Uncle Ben, a retired headmaster
of Durston House Preparatory School for Boys, looked like a
great solemn warlord. So wrote Merton later, describing his
huge white waterfall mustache, his pince-nez glasses, his ill-
fitting tweeds, and his stoop-shouldered carriage. He required
much attention.

Aunt Maud was a gentle being. "I think I have met very
few people in my life so like an angel." Merton described her
as one who remained a Victorian girl, no matter how she
aged. Tall and thin, quiet and meek, she dressed in a mode

that had been fashionable half a century before. Her thin, smiling lips seemed to wish to say nice things and to soften blows. She particularly wanted to do nice things for the lonely, motherless boy who came to the red brick house to stay for a while.

No sooner had Tom arrived than she took him on a shopping expedition in Oxford Street in London. If he was to go to school in England, he ought not look like a foreigner. Off went Tom and Aunt Maud, and she bought him several pairs of gray flannel trousers, a sweater, some shoes, some gray flannel shirts, and one of those floppy flannel hats that English children had to wear.

Riding back to Ealing on top of the open bus, Aunt Maud said conversationally, "I wonder if Tom has thought at all about his future." She addressed him in the third person, probably so she would not sound as if she were prying.

"Do you think writing would be a good profession for anyone?" asked Tom, hesitating to come straight out and say he wished to be a novelist.

"Yes, indeed," Aunt Maud responded, "writing is a very fine profession! But what kind of writing would you like to do?"

Tom admitted he'd like to write stories, and then Aunt Maud said: "I imagine you'd do quite well at that some day. Of course writers sometimes find it very difficult to make their way in the world."

Tom looked dejected and Aunt Maud, not one to foster discouragement, hastened to add: "If you had some other occupation to make a living, you might find time to write in your spare moments. Novelists sometimes get their start that way, you know."

He cheered up. "I might be a journalist and write for newspapers."

Aunt Maud happily concurred and pointed out that Tom was ahead of the writing game because he had a knowledge of languages. "A knowledge of languages is valuable in that field. You could work your way up to the position of a foreign correspondent."

Matching her enthusiasm, Tom added: "And I could write books in my spare time." So he rode home to Ealing with new clothes and high ambitions for a great career for Tom Merton, foreign correspondent who wrote novels in his spare time.

But first he must get through prep school. Prep school was Ripley Court, in Surrey, about thirty miles from London. Mrs. Pearce, the headmistress of Ripley Court, was Aunt Maud's sister-in-law.

Mrs. Pearce was not impressed by Tom, nor by his ambition to be a writer. She was a bulky, belligerent woman. When Tom and Aunt Maud entered her domain, she was standing in a room where several of his father's paintings hung. She would glance from Tom to the paintings, as if to show her grim disapproval of art and artists. Aunt Maud tried to get on her good side and show what a solid boy Tom Merton was by mentioning that they'd been talking about Tom's future.

Mrs. Pearce grunted: "Does he want to be a dilettante like his father?"

Aunt Maud said gently: "We were thinking he might become a journalist."

Mrs. Pearce snorted. "Nonsense. Let him go into business and make a decent living. There's no use his deceiving himself. He might as well get sensible ideas into his head from the very start and prepare himself for something reliable. He can't go out into the world with his head full of dreams." She turned on Tom: "Boy! Don't become a dilettante, do you hear?"

It didn't seem an auspicious start at Ripley Court, yet things weren't too bad. It was lucky he could be accepted at all, since the term was well under way. But, since he was regarded as an orphan—despite the fact that he had a father— allowances were made.

For Mrs. Pearce, the allowances made were vast. In her eyes Tom was suspect just by being the son of an artist. Added to that, he came from a French lycée—that made him a foreigner! To crown it all, here was a boy into his fourteenth year who didn't know Latin!

Once again, as in St. Antonin, Tom had the embarrassment of sitting with the smallest boys in the school, beginning at the beginning again. But there were compensations—Ripley Court was a happy place after the prison of the lycée. Its huge green cricket field, the deep shadows of the elm trees, the dining room where they crammed themselves with bread and butter and jam at teatime while listening to Mr. Onslow reading the works of Sir Arthur Conan Doyle, made for a sense of security.

Tom thought the red-faced innocent English boys were much pleasanter than the ruffians of Montauban. On Sundays, dressed in their black Eton jackets, their snow-white Eton collars choking them up to the chin, they marched off to the village church. For the first time, Tom was going to church, not to gaze at works of art, but as a "churchgoer."

Tom's father used to tell him the stories behind the religious symbols, sculptures, paintings, and stained-glass windows when they visited the ancient churches of southern France. Tom vividly remembered one night—his father and he were standing in the hall of the flat they'd taken in a three-story house at the edge of St. Antonin. They had arrived home late from exploring some ruined churches. As they got off the dawn train, they heard a cock crow. His father began to tell Tom about Peter's betraying Jesus three times before the cock crowed. Entering the hall outside their flat, they stood there while his father finished the story of Peter. Tom never forgot the way his father said: "Peter went out and wept bitterly."

Going to church at Ripley Court was not for that kind of spiritual teaching; it was more a learning of how to be respectable. At Ripley, religion was respectability, learning the code of a gentleman. But there was peace in the orderliness of such a life. Tom enjoyed the long walks in the country on Sunday evenings, as well as going to church on Sunday mornings. Best of all he liked going to the drill room just as darkness fell, to listen to Mr. Onslow read aloud from *Pilgrim's Progress* and to sing hymns.

This was the first time Tom had ever seen people kneel publicly at bedtime. All the boys were expected to kneel by their beds before getting into them. It was also the first time Tom had ever heard grace said publicly before all meals. This was systematic religion, and he was attracted by it. He prayed at all times of the day or night. Later, he referred to those two years as his "religious phase." But that was after he became disillusioned, and found out that English boys could be just as coarse and brutal and vicious as French boys.

The sunny, beautiful English countryside, the green cricket fields, white church spires, the comfort and security of tea-time were only one side of the English scene. The picture had a darker side and underneath the sweetness and light was murk. Side by side with romantic history was the reality of modern industrialism.

At first, London had seemed a city of angels, whose streets were full of happy traffic, red buses, shining cars, and kind men walking with their gloves and their rolled-up umbrellas in the sunlight. It was a brave new world that had such beautiful people in it. Only later did he see the great areas of slums, the slowly dying, the doomed. Then he saw that it was a cowardly old world that had such ugly people in it.

Still, London remained full of excitement. He had London in his system and could not get it out. He became a slave to London, the city where you could be surrounded by people, yet all alone. He would stand and look up at the clear warm sky, or, walk down Piccadilly and see the whores leaning against the buildings. "When the whores called out to me," he wrote later, "I did not laugh with fear or derision. I did not know the difference between life and death then." They were part of the beauty, and they were beautiful.

In two years, Tom was ready to graduate. By that time he had picked up enough learning to make a presentable showing in a scholarship examination. He was particularly influenced by his Latin teacher, a small, thin man, funny and friendly. Thanks to him, Tom got a good grounding in Latin.

One day, Tom met his Latin teacher by chance in London and he took Tom to see a Harold Lloyd movie. They laughed so hard they nearly fell out of the balcony.

Just before the end of the term, Tom's father became seriously ill. Tom went to see him. His father was in bed; he didn't look ill, yet he seemed in pain whenever he moved and he didn't say much. Tom asked if he knew what was wrong with him. His father said that nobody seemed to know.

Tom returned to school to finish out the term, sad and

troubled. He told himself that his father always got better after these strange sieges which nobody seemed to understand. And his father did get better.

When the summer holiday arrived, he told Tom they were going to Scotland together. An old friend of his had a place in Aberdeenshire and had invited him to come and rest and get well. They took the night train from King's Cross. His father seemed fine at first, but by the time they got to Aberdeen, he looked very tired and was too quiet. At last they got to Insch, their host's grouse-moor. The sun was slanting long rays over the hills of heather as they came to the house.

Tom's father went directly to his room and there he stayed. At first he came down for meals, then not even for meals, and one morning he called Tom in and said: "I have to go back to London. I must go to a hospital, son."

Tom couldn't grasp this news at first: "Are you worse?"

"Pray God to make me well," he said. Then, seeing Tom's face, added: "Don't be unhappy, Tom."

But he was terribly unhappy, and when his father went on to say: "You'll stay here. They are very nice and will take care of you. It will do you good. Do you like horses?" Tom didn't answer.

His father was put on the train to London's Middlesex Hospital and Tom was left behind in Scotland's cold summer. His hosts had two nieces, aged sixteen and seventeen, who were also staying at the house that summer. They were passionately devoted to horses, and they bossed fourteen-year-old Tom around and gave him instructions on everything that had to do with horses.

Indeed, Tom's hosts believed horses and horse-grooming would make a man out of this orphan. At dawn he had to be up and in the stables with his pitchfork, cleaning out the stalls of the two ponies. As the new sun came slanting through the pines, the nieces directed Tom. They groomed the horses tirelessly, but Tom just groomed them doggedly.

After grooming the horses they would, at last, assemble for breakfast. The cook and two maids in their pale blue smocks and white aprons came in, at the other end of the dining room. Everyone knelt, faces to the wall, heads in hands, as the Master read a lesson from the Bible and some prayers.

Then the maids silently went out and everybody helped himself from various silver chafing dishes on the sideboard; there was never any ham or bacon because the family was vegetarian.

The two nieces soon saw he was shirking the horse-grooming. That he should be willing to give up the reward of riding the horse just to get out of the task of grooming was incomprehensible, and they realized he was a wrong one. He wasn't British. He had foreign traits—a French sullenness and a Spanish treachery—and so they decided he shouldn't be rewarded with riding any more.

This was exactly what Tom had in mind. He immediately went walking on the moors. With all the horse-grooming and riding, there hadn't been time for walking. He walked through wet heather in the cold wind, to the top of a hill three miles away, and sat on a big stone to think.

Would he ever get back to London? He felt hopeless. He had to stay wherever put until somebody moved him. Yet it wasn't necessary that he should be stuck here with strangers when he had relatives in England and in other parts of the world.

These friends of Tom's father sincerely believed they were doing a work of charity. They believed in doing good for others—providing the others were teachable and worthy. They wanted to do their best for Tom, but that meant getting rid of his bad character traits.

Tom escaped through the escape hatch he'd discovered long ago—books. The two things he liked to do best were reading and writing in his journal. His hosts thought the purpose of reading was to find a moral or to get a sermon out of the story.

On the long summer evenings, the entire family would gather together to sit in the library on straight-backed chairs. There they were read to, from Charles Kingsley's *Water Babies*. The story told of two chimney sweeps who had escaped from industrial civilization into the fairyland of cleanliness and affluence, and the moral of the story was—in case you didn't get it—that if you are tidy and good-mannered others will be nice to you.

One dank foggy afternoon, Tom stole out of the library

with his favorite book, *The Count of Monte Cristo* (in French), on his way to climb a special tree where he could hide in the branches and read, unseen, all day long. But he was caught just at the door.

"I'd like to speak to you," said the lady of the house, and marched him back into the library.

They sat down on the hard chairs, facing each other. Tom kept nervously turning the book over and over in his hands until she said in exasperation: "Stop it!" Then, to make up for her harshness and to show she was his friend, she quickly asked: "Did you ever read *The Jungle Book*, by Rudyard Kipling?"

"Yes," said Tom, sensing he was in for one more moral homily.

"Do you remember who Mowgli was?"

He had a wonderful memory, almost total recall, and remembered in detail the story of Mowgli, brought up by the wolves, taught the laws and ways of the jungle by Baloo, the bear, and by Bagheera, the black panther.

"He was a boy who lived wild in the jungle with animals; he lived away from people; he was wild," responded Tom stoutly.

This was not the answer she wanted and quickly she said: "Did he live alone?" strongly emphasizing the word *alone*. But before Tom could speak, she provided the answer to her question herself. "No, of course not. Nobody can live alone. We all have to depend on one another. Mowgli lived with a pack of wolves. Why do you suppose the wolves and Mowgli got along together?"

Tom got his answer in fast. "Because he liked the wolves and they liked him, they got along, they were like brothers."

"First came duty," she said severely, then asked with stern face: "What duty?"

He didn't know. He couldn't remember anything in the book about duty, he just thought they got along because they liked each other.

"Duty!" she admonished. "Duty held them together, the duty to run with the pack. The pack came first. Run with the pack. Hunt with the group. Everybody depends on everybody else. Everybody does his bit. Mowgli had his part to play, too." She paused for breath, then plowed on. "It is like *The Three Musketeers*. Do you remember what kept them together?"

Tom had to admit he remembered their motto—"all for one and one for all." She scored her point. But even after he'd shown he understood, she still couldn't stop.

"Of course you know that the Indian Civil Service is one of the hardest services in the world to get into," she continued. "I used to know a young man who was like you, knew many languages, was also very clever. However, he had one terrible fault. He sulked. They sent him to India and he made a wonderful career for himself in India. And remember"—she looked Tom in the eye—"there isn't a man in either of the universities that wouldn't give anything for the chance to be in the Indian Civil. That shows you are among the most brilliant men in the world. But this man, brilliant as he was, had this one fault. He sulked. He did not run with the pack. So one of the army men gave him a good talking to. And what did he do? Went off by himself on his horse into the jungle, and"—she paused dramatically, and then said: "and—he was never seen again! Went off in a sulk and never heard of again—a brilliant man, perhaps eaten by a tiger! All from sulking!"

At last she let him go. He ran out of the house, climbed the cedar with its roomy branches. Hours passed. He was the Count of Monte Cristo, tied in a sack, hiding inside with a knife, thrown for dead over the high bastions of the Chateau d'If into the sea.

Many years later, after he had become a monk and a hermit, Thomas Merton wrote that he had chosen the direction his soul would take during that summer of his youth. The direction was toward *beingness*. In many essays and books written when he grew older, he affirmed over and over again that a person did not have to justify the right to read a book, or just to be idle and listen.

"Can't I just be in the woods without any special reason?" he wrote. "Just being in the woods at night, in the cabin, is something too excellent to be justified or explained. It just *is*." And he told of listening to the rain: "Think of it: all

that speech pouring down, selling nothing, judging nobody. . . ."

He never forgot his experiences during that holiday in
Scotland.

The summer dragged on. The family gave up on Tom. He
was left more and more alone.

One day in the deserted house the telephone rang. He sat
and let it ring, absorbed in his book. It went on ringing and
ringing. At last he answered it, annoyed. The operator said
there was a telegram for Thomas Merton. He couldn't make
out her Scotch brogue, but at last she got through to him.
The wire said:

"Entering New York harbor. All well."

It was signed "Father" and had been sent from the hospital in London. Tom argued with the operator. The telegram
couldn't say "Entering New York harbor" and be addressed
from the hospital in London. The operator said the message
was correctly read by her and that was what it said.

Tom hung up. He walked up and down, up and down.
The silence and emptiness of the house pressed in on him.
What was happening to his father in that London hospital?

Uncle Ben told him when Tom entered the house at
Ealing: "Your father has a malignant tumor on the brain."

In the hospital, his father lay in a dimly lit ward. Now that
Tom talked to him, he felt a wave of reassurance. It was not
as he'd feared from the telegram. His father was lucid; he was
not out of his mind.

His father said they were going to try to operate, but they
were afraid they couldn't do much. He asked Tom to pray.

How, Tom wondered, should he pray? He recalled his father reading the poems of William Blake to him when he
was ten. Now he wished his father could read Blake aloud
once again, and they could talk about it. He longed to reach
out to his father spiritually—especially as his father had asked
him to pray. He could not say the pious prayers of English
schoolboys in Eton collars, intoning in church. There was another kind of prayer. It was Blake's, and to Blake he must go.

4

*I suddenly remembered all the times I had sat waiting
in movie houses . . . waiting for the picture to start.*

September came. Uncle Ben had suggested that Oakham was
the best choice for Tom's next school. Oakham was a very
decent school with an old tradition and a good rating and it
was not as expensive as the great public schools like Harrow
and Winchester. Also, the scholarship exams at Harrow and
Winchester would have been too difficult for Tom. So Oakham it was.

Tom began at the top; that is, he lived in the garret. The
garret-dwellers were a sorry lot who breathed stale air, tried to
study by gaslight, fought, shouted, strummed the one ukulele
among the eight of them, and on weekends, or whenever
food arrived, ate themselves sick on potato chips and raisin
wine.

Tom would escape outdoors. Only outdoors could he be
quiet and think, study, read, or write. He walked the long
steep streets, climbed to the top of Brooke Hill, and there he
sat on a stile, reading, or just looking over the countryside.

Oakham was ninety-four miles from London. As there was
no main railway line, Oakham was truly an isolated, peaceful

place with its fourteenth-century church, from whose steeple the bells intoned the time of day and night.

In December, Tom moved downstairs into the Upper Fifth. The new study had more light, but it was just as crowded and messy, and he went on walking up Brooke Hill to ponder and to study.

He was fifteen that January of 1930, and a new decade, the thirties, was opening. It was to be very different from the lifestyle that marked the twenties, symbolized, more or less, in the popular dance called the Charleston.

The change from frantic cynicism was heralded almost the instant the new decade began by one of the most singular personalities ever to challenge the British Empire.

Mahatma Gandhi was a dark-skinned man who set forth to cross the Dandi desert of India on foot, naked except for a loincloth. He was going to make salt, openly defying British law and confronting the Western world with the simple truth that his people, under affluent British rule, were dying in horrible poverty.

In faraway Oakham, the students heard of Gandhi. How could they avoid it when the angry English press was telling them every day how outrageous it was that the Christian Rectitude of Englishmen should be challenged by this Black, by "a naked fakir."

Most of the boys of Oakham agreed. They made loud derisive noises when they saw the nearly naked Mahatma pictured in the paper. Except Tom. He was for Gandhi and argued fiercely with the other boys.

That desperate summer in Scotland had started a counterforce in Tom's spirit. His own rebellion had been minor, but it had strengthened his determination not to conform to his peers just because they were his peers, nor to his superiors just because they were his superiors. Yet he was always polite in his resistance, just as Gandhi was. Such resistance, no matter how polite, could get you into deep trouble. But he had learned one thing—nonviolence had to be for something strongly believed; it couldn't be negative and passive, arising out of cowardice.

Out of his espousal of Mahatma Gandhi at age fifteen grew his passionate resolution to stand up for peace all his

life. Later, writing of Gandhi, he described him as the first of
the modern men of the twentieth century called to the special task of enlightenment of the soul.

Gandhi exploded the Kipling platitude that East is East
and West is West and never the twain shall meet. The
Mahatma, brought up in a strict orthodox Hindu caste, had
been a student in England. Later, in South Africa, he read
the Bible and was moved by the Sermon on the Mount to
say that Christian and Hindu beliefs are harmonious. Gandhi
explained: "Jesus died in vain if he did not teach us to regu-
late the whole of life by the eternal law of love." Tom got
the idea—Truth was Love!

This concept of Truth as Love and of Jesus dying for Love
was not exactly the way religion was taught at Oakham. The
chaplain, a witty and sporting Cambridge man, usually ended
religious instruction by sitting on the table and showing the
boys how to row. He didn't think this irrelevant to religious
teaching, because he believed in Christianity as good sportsmanship. That was what religion was for, to teach boys how
to be gentlemen.

"If I talk with the tongues of men and of angels, and be
not a gentleman, I am become as sounding brass," was the
way he read the thirteenth chapter of First Corinthians.

Tom went and looked it up. What the text really said was:
"If I talk with the tongues of men and of angels, and have
not *charity*, I am become as sounding brass."

When challenged, the chaplain explained that the word
"gentleman" is the word for "charity," because charity is
good sportsmanship; charity is playing the game according to
the rules; charity is working with the team; it's cricket; it's
not being a cad or a bounder.

Tom waited for the chaplain to proclaim the apocalyptic
sentence of that thirteenth chapter of First Corinthians—
"Now there remain faith, hope, and charity, and the greatest
of these is charity"—as "Now there remain faith, hope, and
gentlemanliness, and the greatest of these is gentlemanliness." But the chaplain never did. By the time he reached
that sentence he was up on the table, showing the boys how
to row.

June came. Tom had learned a great deal that first year at

Oakham. He was reading Chaucer, Shakespeare, Cicero, and most of all, William Blake.

In June, Pop and Bonnemaman and John Paul came from America to be near Tom's father. They took a place in London close to the hospital and each day they went to visit the sick man. When Tom looked at his father, he knew he could not live much longer. "How are you, Father?"

His father put out his hand, and Tom realized his father could no longer speak. But his eyes told Tom that he knew them all, and that his mind was clear.

The sorrow of his father's inability to communicate with them, the pathos of his father's helplessness, crushed Tom. Despite all his training to keep a stiff upper lip, his lips trembled, his eyes filled with tears, and he bent down and hid his face in the blanket. The others, helpless to do anything, looked on in tears.

The long sad summer wore on. Day after day they went to the hospital. One afternoon Tom found his father's bed covered with little sheets of blue notepaper on which he'd drawn Byzantine saints. They looked excited, angry, wore long beards, and had great halos. He had never made drawings like that before. Behind the wall of his isolation, he was intensely alive in the spirit.

"Of us all," wrote Tom afterward, "Father was the only one who really had any kind of faith."

Summer turned into fall and Tom made ready to go back to Oakham. The family decided that in the year ahead Tom should spend more holidays with his godfather in London. An old friend of Tom's father from New Zealand, Dr. Tom Bennet was a prestigious physician, a "Harley Street" specialist.

In his novel, *My Argument With the Gestapo*, Merton writes an impressionistic remembrance of those great vacations in the London flat of his godfather: "There I woke up in the mornings of Easter vacations with the quiet light of London coming in the two curtained windows"—and breakfast coming to his bed, coffee or chocolate in a tiny pot, toast or rolls, and fresh eggs. Breakfast didn't come in until nine in the morning, so Tom stayed in bed reading. His godfather was a great influence on him, introducing Tom to modern novels, modern art, and great music. He encouraged the boy to be sharply perceptive. Once Tom argued with his godfather that Ravel's *Bolero* was not phony, as his godfather had said. But next time he heard the *Bolero* he knew it was phony indeed.

With devoted generosity, Tom's godfather was grooming his godson for the role of a career diplomat. He therefore encouraged Tom to go abroad during holidays, to learn the languages and customs of other countries. The English diplomatic service liked knowledgeable, civilized, cosmopolitan persons, sensitive to art, literature, and the history of civilizations. During the holidays Tom spent in his godfather's flat, the poetry of English literature, the pageantry of English history, and the best of English civility were served to him on a silver platter.

But the boy who was captured by the heroic actions of Mahatma Gandhi was not a person who would be satisfied with the comforts of material wealth, no matter the sense of security such comforts bring. On other levels, English life was not cultured, nor civil, nor filled with pageantry. When the mask fell off, there was revealed a raw wound of suffering.

One of Tom's friends at Oakham was the son of a country parson in the Isle of Wight. Andrew wore horn-rimmed spectacles and a lock of his black hair fell down over his forehead. He was one of the school intellectuals, and he and Tom would sit together in the library at Oakham, surrounded by walls of books, talking in whispers of other than intellectual subjects and sipping a purple concoction called Vimto. They kept the bottle hidden under the table.

One holiday, Tom went home with Andrew; he was sixteen at the time. Andrew's family lived in the rectory and the nearest village was three or four miles if you walked over the downs, but seven or eight miles by road.

The Isle of Wight was rainier than ever that year, and they were bored. Then a movie came to the village, and the parson said he'd take them all to the movies on the bus—Andrew, Tom, and Andrew's little sister. As they were practically addicted to movies, their anticipation was immense.

The movie house turned out to be a corrugated iron shed, where they sat on rickety, squeaking seats. Tom suddenly felt deflated. What if the movie wasn't any good? All his life he'd sat in movie houses, waiting for the picture to start, praying it would be a good movie. He'd grown up on movies.

His grandfather had originated the idea of printing books about popular movies, illustrated with stills from the films. When Tom was living with his grandparents, Pop often took him to the publishing house where he worked, Grosset & Dunlap. There Tom would curl up in a leather armchair, surrounded by movie books, and read all day.

"I really hope it will be a good picture," he whispered to Andrew's little sister. But as soon as the movie started, the kids realized it was going to be terrible and they got up and walked out, emerging into the rainy street, pale, bleary-eyed, and sick, as if the movie had been so awful it destroyed their health.

Suddenly, Tom recognized a girl he knew. She was with another group walking out of the movie, a slender girl with large, thoughtful, rather abstract eyes. He'd only met her once, two years ago, and never seen her again until now—but that one time they'd met had been an unforgettable afternoon.

It was during that summer of his discontent in Scotland. His hosts had taken the nieces and Tom to visit some friends for tennis and tea. The friends had nieces, too. This girl was one of their nieces. She and Tom were the youngest at the party and they were left to each other. Soon it became clear they'd be the last to get a tennis court, since courts were assigned in order of seniority—as good British form demanded. The girl's uncle and aunt, with Tom's hosts and the two sets of older nieces, had to play before the younger ones could. Tom and the girl sat together; they sat and they sat, and they sat. No one got tired and gave up a court to them. All afternoon they sat side by side.

At last, muscles stiff and aching from their long time sitting, they got up, abandoned the tennis courts, and walked about in the flower garden.

Finally it was teatime. The girl's uncle, called the Captain, had been to see *The Jazz Singer*, and couldn't get over how

amazing and remarkable this film was—it was the first talkie!
But the guests sneered, as nothing was more beneath them
than an American movie. However, the Captain persisted
earnestly: "You would never criticize the cinema again if you
could hear that voice!"

At this, the Captain's wife, fearing her cultured guests
would look down on all of them when it was the Captain
alone who showed such "vulgar" taste, exclaimed with a little
laugh: "Can you imagine him, poor dear? He wept and wept
and wept and wept when the Jew sang!"

Tom and the girl exchanged glances, realizing with tele-
pathic understanding that they had a lot in common. They
slid out of their chairs and slipped away.

"I saw the picture, too," she whispered to him, "and I
thought it was frightfully silly." Walking off together, they
began to talk humorously about movies.

Now, as if fate had ordained it, they were meeting once
more over a silly movie. If they hadn't walked out in the middle of the picture, they might never have met again!

She looked straight at Tom, and he went directly up and
spoke to her as if two years hadn't passed at all. He had never
felt this deep harmony with a girl; it was as if they'd known
each other always.

All the friends around them wanted to be introduced, and
soon they were using up all the time they had together introducing everyone to everyone else. Andrew immediately fell
for her and kept pestering Tom: "Who is she? Who is she?"
Even after Tom explained, Andrew kept on: "Where does
she come from? Did you know her well? Did you go together? Where does she go to school? When do you see each
other?"

Tom hadn't known this girl at all, except for that one afternoon; yet it didn't seem strange that everyone assumed
they were old friends.

At last the parson quieted his excited son because he realized that this girl must be staying at the Admiral's. Well, he
knew the Admiral, so he assured his son, and Tom too, that
there was no fear they'd lose sight of her.

Not long after, they all received an invitation to a fancy-costume party at the Admiral's. As the parson had no car, they hired a taxi, and off they went, dressed in borrowed finery. Andrew wore a brown friar's habit he'd managed to pick up, and Tom borrowed some riding breeches, boots, and a sombrero. He announced that he was a horse thief. Andrew's little sister wore a big hoop skirt and said she was a shepherdess.

The moment they arrived, Tom began looking for "his" girl, and immediately she appeared out of the crowd, dressed as a gypsy. "May I have this dance?" he said, forgetting he couldn't dance, just wanting to take her hand, and also wanting to get her away from Andrew.

"Yes," she said, and they started across the floor.

Both realized what they'd forgotten—neither of them could dance. She tripped over his feet, he stepped on hers. He said: "My fault," and tried to joke about everybody's crazy costumes, until finally the music stopped. He saw her to the edge of the dance floor, then went to another room to pull himself together. There, older people offered him some port, but the wine was too sweet, and when he finished drinking it, he felt depressed.

He came out into the hall and there on the stairs was Andrew with Tom's girl—he'd taken the opportunity to capture her, and they had their heads together, talking in serious whispers. Tom came over and said hello.

They looked up at him briefly, said hello, and then turned back to each other and their own serious conversation. Tom walked away, feeling disgusted with himself, wondering why he'd thought this silly outfit would be interesting. The floor was full of kids dressed like cowboys.

He pulled off his cowboy scarf, ditching it and his sombrero in the closet. Then he went into the library and just sat. Time passed. A couple of men came in and wanted to use the library.

Tom went out into the hall again, and glancing up saw that there was no one on the stairs. His heart gave a great thump.

At that moment the parson came up and said he was getting all their raincoats together because they were leaving. Tom drooped.

"Do you wish to stay longer?" the parson asked. Tom nodded, so they all said their good-bys except Tom. He hurried away into the other room where he'd spotted his girl. She was standing by the window, looked more bored than ever. She was alone. She turned and looked at him, and moved toward him. Then she was in his arms and they were dancing. They didn't step on each other's toes; they were dancing as if they had always been beautiful dancers and were only waiting to find each other. Tom knew he loved her more than the whole world.

She was not like any of the other girls he was always falling for; yet, in a way, he knew that when he loved a girl, he always thought each one was different.

But she really *was* different. There was nothing phony about her. She was bored at masquerades, and so was he. They agreed to see each other as often as possible.

By the time the Christmas holidays came, Tom's godfather recognized that Tom had become too intense over this sixteen-year-old girl: it wasn't sensible for a boy intended for a career diplomat. His godfather arranged for Tom to go to Strasbourg and stay in a German *pension* so that he could become more fluent in languages. He spent Christmas there, away from home and family and friends.

On his way back to Oakham he stopped in London to see his father. A week later the headmaster called him into his study and handed him a telegram. His father was dead. He reread the telegram and tried to grasp what had happened. Here was a man. Here was a man with a wonderful mind and a great talent and a great heart. This man had brought Tom into the world and nourished and cared for him and had shaped his soul—here was a man, killed by a growth on his brain.

Tom returned to Oakham after the funeral in London, feeling empty, not even caring to read Blake anymore. But Blake was part of his father and so Blake was part of Tom. One gray Sunday after the long winter of emptiness, Tom walked alone out Brooke Road and up the bare hogback hill called Brooke Hill. Sitting on the stile he repeated some lines of Blake he had memorized:

> "The atoms of Democritus
> And Newton's particles of Light
> Are sands upon the Red Sea shore
> Where Israel's tents do shine so bright."

Suddenly he felt good. The empty feeling was gone.

Pop wrote asking Tom to come to America that summer. Tom bought a new suit and sailed away over the Atlantic. It was on this trip he was bedazzled by the coquette twice his age who still managed to give the impression of being sixteen.

"That devouring, emotional, passionate love of adolescence that sinks its claws into you and consumes you day and night and eats into the vitals of your soul!"

Bonnemaman, Tom's grandmother, had been looking forward to Tom's being home with them in Douglaston. She hoped this would be their chance to know each other better, have interesting conversations, and go places together.

But Tom didn't want to be with his family at all. He just wanted to roam the streets of New York, go to movies, smoke cigarettes, and think. Bonnemaman, sadly disappointed, waited each night for him to come home, hoping they would talk and come to know each other. He saw little of her or of his grandfather. When he wasn't roaming the city streets, he was reading all night on the cool sleeping porch, while summer moths batted against the screen trying to get into the light. Sometimes the family tried to find out what he was reading. When they glanced at the titles of the books by Hemingway, D. H. Lawrence, Aldous Huxley, and the Communist pamphlets that now fascinated him, they went away arching their eyebrows, more bewildered than ever.

Back at Oakham, it was his last year. He was House Prefect in Hodge Wing; one of the lords, top man. He hung his own pictures on the walls of his big study—prints by Manet, photographs from museums—and, on his shelves went all the avant-garde books—novels, poetry, Marx's *Communist Manifesto*, and Baudelaire. He also had room for his Duke Ellington records and played them day and night.

Again, at holiday time, his godfather urged him to go to Germany, to improve his facility in the language. At Koblenz, Tom felt sick. An infection was developing under one of his toenails. He decided to ignore it. By the time he got back to Oakham, he had a bad toothache, too.

The school dentist looked at Tom's teeth and said the infected tooth must come out. He said he couldn't give Tom anything to deaden the pain because there was too much infection. Then he took his forceps and pulled. Tom felt one vivid flash of pain. The tooth was out and he was spitting pus and blood into the blue pool of water beside the dentist's chair.

He walked wearily back to school. By nightfall he was achingly ill and running a high temperature. The school doctor came and immediately said gangrene was setting in and they would have to lance a hole in Tom's gum to drain out the pockets of infection, which meant he had to go to the infirmary.

In the infirmary, the doctor gave him a little ether and the gum was lanced; then Tom slept. He awoke with a mouth full of pus and instinctively knew he had blood poisoning. Sick to death with pain and nausea and a sensation that pus was filling him, he saw the angel of death come and stand, a dark shadow, beside his bed.

He kept his eyes closed. He would not look at Death. He was too tired, too sick. "Come on," he whispered. "If I have to die—let me die, then." He felt his life was finished and he didn't care. Then he fell asleep.

Next day he was sent off to the school sanitarium and there he was doctored and nursed until, despite his death wish, he began to get better. His friends and family, including his godfather, knew Tom was getting better because he began writing a long essay on the modern novel. He wrote it as he recovered and he won the Bailey English Prize for it. Seventeen years old. He began to revive and to play his records—the hottest and loudest—while the other students were grinding over the syntax of Virgil's *Georgics*.

His headmaster brought him a book of the poems of Gerard Manley Hopkins, and he read them curiously. He'd never heard of this Catholic poet who was also a Jesuit priest.

As he read, he wasn't sure he liked a poet with that kind of originality, and most of all, he wasn't sure he approved of that kind of mysticism.

By the time he came out of the sanitarium, it was time to work for the big exams. He and Andrew studied together. Tom took the exams in French and German and Latin at the end of June. The results came out in September: Andrew had failed; Tom had made it. But they were determined to go up to Cambridge together.

In the dank mists of December, he and Andrew went up to Cambridge to sit for the scholarship exam. All that week Tom sat under the high rafters at Trinity College and covered long sheets of paper with essays on Molière, Racine, Balzac, Victor Hugo, Goethe, and so forth. At last it was over. They looked in the *Times.* Both Andrew and he had succeeded; Andrew was to go to St. Catherine's and Tom to Clare College.

He was finished with Oakham. He had his independence. But underneath the knowledgeable young man, he was the same boy who waited in tense anticipation for the movie to start, staring at the white screen, hoping it would be a good show and that, this time, he would meet the great adventure of life, meet "The midnight express/Bringing Plato, . . . Milton, Blake. . . ."

5

"There is a grain of sand in Lambeth which Satan cannot find."

The results of the scholarship exam came out at the end of December. A few weeks later, on January 31, he was eighteen, and his godfather treated him to a celebration of both events—the scholarship achievement and his birthday. It was an unforgettable champagne supper.

As Tom would not be entering Cambridge until the fall, he had a seven-month vacation ahead. He was off for Italy. When he got to Genoa, he was out of money and wrote his godfather asking for more. His godfather, guardian of Tom's finances, was displeased and took this opportunity to call attention to Tom's lack of intelligence about money. Not only did he reprimand Tom for the way he was squandering his funds, he went on to speak of the way he was dissipating himself, pointing out Tom's faults in detail.

His godfather's disapproval was more than just a scolding. Tom's whole idea of success was derived from him and he wanted to do what would please his godfather.

He recalled all the things he'd learned from his godfather. Thanks to him, Tom had been given a chance to develop his own critical perceptions, without having to conform to mediocrity or to the shallow, middle-class standards of his society. He didn't have to pretend to admire the things he thought were not admirable. He didn't have to praise British royalty, or pretend he agreed that horses made for a really right person.

If he made a list of the things he'd learned from his godfather, it would include the most intellectual, as well as the most modern, literary works—Balzac, Flaubert, Hemingway, Dos Passos, D. H. Lawrence, James Joyce. The list would contain avant-garde artists of all kinds, the films of René Clair and the Russians, the music of Stravinsky and Scriabin, even the right kinds of wines to order.

Then there were the trips abroad all during his years at Oakham, with letters of introduction to the great German professors, which his godfather obtained so that Tom could have entry into the most educated, intelligent, artistic, and philosophic circles.

Only from his father had Tom learned more—but it was a totally different dimension of learning. From his father he learned about Blake and Gregorian music, Byzantine art and Dante, and the story of St. Peter's denial of Christ. From his teachers, too, he had learned things he didn't owe to his godfather. He'd learned the Greek and Latin poets, whose philosophic thoughts Tom would ponder and find valid years hence.

He was grateful to his teachers at Oakham for this learning, because it helped him to know the wholeness of his civilization—not just James Joyce and Hemingway, D. H. Lawrence and Celine, but also the words of Virgil in the *Georgics*. The works of the moderns were filled with the roar of the river of hell. The works of the ancients were filled with the silence of seeing into "the root of things," thus conquering fear and fate.

In his quest for truth, it was years before he found the solitude, silence, and meditation necessary for seeing into the root of things which the *Georgics* described as the only reason for knowledge. First he had to go through that roaring river of hell.

The displeasure of his godfather made Tom feel worthless.

He felt that he was not a good character and that depressed him. Also, he had a boil on his elbow and a sickening toothache. The old blood-poisoning was starting again, and maybe it didn't matter all that much whether he lived or died. Nevertheless, in Rome he went to a dentist. The dentist gave him some ether, and when Tom woke up, the dentist was waving the red, abscessed roots of his tooth in Tom's face.

After that Tom began slowly to heal, but his depression remained. He wandered around the ruins of imperial Rome, bored, and at night he went home to read D. H. Lawrence and James Joyce.

One day he wandered into the Church of Sts. Cosmas and Damian to look at the art treasures. The instant he stepped inside something hit him, an exhilaration like a current of electricity. The great mosaic of Christ coming in judgment had a burning impact beyond mere aesthetics. Tom began to haunt the churches.

One night, reading some poems of D. H. Lawrence containing symbols and prophecies based on Ezekiel and the Apocalypse, he sensed a false note. He looked up the prophets in the Vulgate Bible and found that the Apocalyptic purity was a kind of truthfulness very different from Lawrence's pretentiousness. He tossed the book of poems across the room. How could he have fallen for that phony blood-mystique?

Another night, Tom's father appeared to him. He had been dead for more than a year, but his presence was as real and as startling as if he had taken Tom by the arm and looked into his eyes. Then the whole thing passed in a flash. Tom put his face in his hands and cried. He went to bed still weeping, but in the morning his depression had vanished for the first time since the day his godfather had chastised him. Tom was filled with good cheer, which lasted for the remainder of his stay in Italy.

Before he left, he took a bus tour through the low hills south of the Tiber, to the Trappist monastery of Tre Fontane. He visited the old church but wouldn't go into the monastery because, he said, he didn't want to see a bunch of monks flagellating themselves with whips, as all the tourists assured him that was what monks did. So he walked up and down under the eucalyptus trees. An odd thought popped into his head: "I should like to become a Trappist monk."

He told this to a student from the American Academy who was riding on the bus with his mother. Horrified, the woman stared at him. Tom realized this was a good way to shock people, if you were in a mood to shock people.

After leaving Italy, he spent the summer at the house in Douglaston. He made the return crossing to England on the cabin-class steamer *Manhattan*. To all appearances, he was the portrait of the artist as a young man of the early thirties. He held his cigarette between his lips, a drink in his hand, and he even wore his hat like Humphrey Bogart.

The voyage was a violent one, marked by drunkenness, fights, jealousies over shipboard love affairs, and scandals. Some of the ship's stewards were Nazis and they detested the passengers they thought were Jews.

This wasn't Tom's first experience with the Nazi mentality. His first experience had come a bit earlier, when he'd gone on a walking tour through the Rhine Valley, a pack on his back. He was walking down a peaceful country road on a Sunday morning. On all sides the apple orchards were flowering. Then a car came very fast, straight at him. By sheer luck he jumped into a ditch as the car went by without altering its course, with him as the target. As it passed, a cloud of leaflets showered over him and he glimpsed the six or seven youths screaming and shaking their fists. It was election day and they were campaigning for Hitler.

Later, he was to write, "They were future officers in the SS. . . . They vanished quickly. The road was once again perfectly silent and peaceful. But it was not the same road as before. It was now a road on which seven men had expressed their readiness to destroy me."

The ship that carried him back to England was just like that. It was the right start for a wrong journey.

The school year began in the gloom of English autumn. Tom started on a downward course and kept on going until he reached bottom. What he afterward remembered about Cambridge was a few moments of elation and a lot of misery. He had only to play his favorite Duke Ellington records to be transported back to the cellar shop, or to the nights he went reeling back to his quarters from The Lion, his favorite pub. And he remembered the mornings after, peering drearily at the gray unwashed windowpanes and listening to the dried scraps of putty fall from the old windows onto the linoleum floor.

His friend Mike, a beefy, red-faced, noisy youth who liked to eat and to chase after girls with hard-breathing passion, killed himself. Tom heard about it after he left Cambridge. Mike was found hanging in the showers, from a rope slung over one of the pipes, his big hearty face black with the agony of strangulation.

"Cambridge you are as quiet as teashops . . . as blue as clinics . . . you are as disquieting as syphilis or cancer," Merton wrote.

He felt that Cambridge symbolized the truth of London, of England, where, under the ancient rites of civilization, a vile body of wounds and injustices lay hidden and suffering.

"The whores in ermine marched out of the doorways, in the dark . . . then suddenly you realized that the fog was hiding the cries . . . of men dying of dope . . . you wondered what perversions . . . behind curtained windows. . . ."

He had heavy dates. One was a girl every freshman worthy of manhood had to date. She was known as "the freshman's delight." Tom took her to see Marlene Dietrich in *The Song of Songs*. Later, after he'd taken her home, he went back to his favorite pub, got drunk, came in late and was gated (grounded) for ten days.

This was the second time he was gated that year, but this time he didn't mind. That first time hurt. His Aunt Maud had died. It was November, just two months after he'd got established at Cambridge. Back in Ealing for her funeral, sadness filled him at the sight of Uncle Ben, sitting in his wheelchair, his face uncomprehending. He kept looking at Tom. He wasn't able to speak, only his eyes sought Tom's, seeming to say: "Why are you doing this to me? Why is everybody trying to tell me Maud is dead?"

There was a "pebble of Jerusalem" in Ealing. He would always feel it—like walking with a stone in your shoe. He would never go back again to Ealing where the most lovely vision of England had been presented to him through the innocent eyes of his aunt.

"They committed the thin body of my poor Victorian angel to the clay of Ealing, and buried my childhood with her."

It was late when the last train took him back to Cambridge, and he fell asleep exhausted and went past his station. He had to turn back. So he got in long after midnight and was gated. He learned with youthful bitterness the kind of justice and compassion that was Cambridge. Like the ship he'd come back on—it was the way things had been going since his godfather had ripped into him during last winter's Italian excursion.

Spring. His godfather was again getting distasteful reports about his godson. Tom, in turn, again heard critical expressions from his godfather. And, after the second time he was gated, a very curt note arrived summoning Tom to The Reckoning. He went.

His godfather kept him waiting, as part of his plan to punish Tom by sapping his morale. After an hour and a half, there wasn't much left of Tom's jaunty spirit, or his capacity to ad-lib his way out of accusations of rotten conduct.

Finally, he was summoned to report, up the narrow turning stairs to his godfather's consulting room. Coolly, almost contemptuously, his godfather offered him a cigarette, implying he was going to need it. Tom refused. The fifteen or twenty minutes that followed were the most painful of his life. It was not just what his godfather said, but it was the cold and disgusted way he said it, his dismissal of Tom as unworthy of all they'd been doing for him. The way he asked Tom to explain his actions already said that nothing could explain such vile conduct. Judgment was passed in advance, because no explanation could possibly justify such a sinner, no matter what he offered. So all Tom offered was contrition. He was sorry, sorry, sorry. That was all he could say, over and over; sorry he'd made so many mistakes.

At last he was out of there. Then he lit a cigarette, walking up the street. No use trying to make up for everything now. It was over. He had messed things up beyond hope.

After the Easter vacation, his tutor called Tom in to ask why he had stopped attending the lectures, wanting to know what had come over an intelligent, sensitive, and promising young person like Tom. Professor Bullough was the one good thing Thomas Merton got out of Cambridge.

A tall, thin, ascetic scholar, Bullough taught him Dante. They had begun in the winter term with the *Inferno*. Taking part of a canto each day, they had followed Dante and Virgil through the icy heart of hell, where the three-headed devil chewed great traitors, then climbed out to the peaceful sea at the foot of the seven-circled mountain of purgatory. From Dante, Merton would later take the title for his powerful autobiography, *The Seven Storey Mountain*. It was Dante's mountain, the seven-circled mountain of purgatory.

Because of this one inspiring and kindly professor, Tom planned to come back next year. He would show his godfather he could make good. He had already arranged for a room in the Old Court of Clare, right over the gate that led out to Clare Bridge. But something told him he never would go to Cambridge again as a member of the university.

His godfather made sure of that. After Tom left for New York, he sent him a letter saying Tom had better give up the idea of entering the British diplomatic service. He said he thought Cambridge was a waste of Tom's time and money and he had better not come back at all. Stay in America.

His godfather had introduced him to the modern novels from which he'd learned that questions of right and wrong didn't exist. The search for pleasure was what was applauded —but when Tom quite simply put what he'd learned into practice, that was unforgivable.

"I found out that, in practice, I was not able to realize how much my pleasures might hurt somebody else until too late. But I didn't know how to say so, because problems of right and wrong didn't exist, as everybody knew. We were merely put on earth to enjoy ourselves without hurting anybody else."

Time to say good-by. There was a royal wedding (Prince George was marrying Princess Marina of Greece) and London was crowded. The train from Cambridge was full of people from the country carrying baskets of food. All along Piccadilly people were lining up, most of them since dawn, sitting on their camp stools.

He telephoned his good-bys. He should call his godfather; then he decided not to call because there wasn't time. Still, he did take a handful of change upstairs to the lounge where the telephone stood, and put the coins in and dialed the number. The words were already shaped on his tongue: "Rushing through London. Afraid I must apologize for saying good-by this way, apologize for everything else too, sorry about Cambridge, good-by." But the telephone rang and nobody answered, so he hung up.

"I wanted to say I was sorry, but the word sorry is the one you use when you step on someone's foot in the bus. I wanted to confess that I had done wrong, but confession is ill bred, and embarrassing for everyone concerned in it. . . . I wanted to say I had sinned, but there was no such thing as sin: sin was a morbid concept, and if you had it in your mind . . . it would poison you and you would go crazy."

Once more, on a ten-day boat out of London, he was outward bound, going through the Straits of Dover. The sun glistened on the white cliffs. Someone said to him:

"What are you going to do in America?"

Sardonically he smiled. "I'm not sure what I'll do in America, perhaps I'll go to Nevada and become the owner of a mine . . . or attend the New School for Social Research and develop a sense of responsibility."

The humor had gone sour.

Yet there was laughter somewhere, a different kind. The rivers of life were flowing; the winds were blowing, his lungs were filling with fresh air.

6

Why I have a wet footprint on top/of my mind

Down wind and down rain and down sleet, Tom came out of
the subway at 116th Street seeking admission to Columbia
University. It was winter and he was twenty.

The campus lay under piles of snow glittering in the cold
sunlight. Morningside Heights smelled sooty, acrid, the air
was biting. None of the students wore an old school tie, or a
blazer, or baggy tweeds, or riding breeches. Columbia could
not afford such academic rites or displays of status; its students were without status or rank. They were "the masses."
They were mostly the children of the middle class, scions of
working people and poor professionals.

The masses! That was the theme song of the thirties. Humanity was on the march, presenting its historic claim to economic justice.

All his life, Tom had heard the still sad music of humanity. When he wandered the streets of London and Paris, he
saw the stark difference between the well-toothed middle
class and the rotten teeth of the needy poor. Four years before, he'd read the *Communist Manifesto* and he'd been pon-

dering it ever since. He went to Russian movies, listened to revolutionary harangues.

Columbia students freely proclaimed radical ideas. They argued, orated, shouted, and marched. "Compared with Cambridge, this big sooty factory was full of light and fresh air. There was a kind of genuine intellectual vitality in the air."

Characteristically, Tom headed for the library, newly built and glowing with bright, shiny lights. There he was told he could take out all the books he wanted. Columbia made him feel that the library, the classes, the distinguished faculty, were all there just for him. This attitude of generosity turned him on "like a pinball machine," and he would come out of the library staggering and nearly hidden behind the load of books in his arms. Blake, Aquinas, Augustine, Eckhart, Coomaraswamy, Hopkins, Maritain—even the French prophetic writer, Léon Bloy, was there.

Sophomores were required to take "Contemporary Civilization," an orientation course. Tom did not look forward to it, imagining that this was just the kind of superficial survey he abhorred. As it happened, this was the course that introduced him to Mark Van Doren, and Mark Van Doren was a teacher with a most profound effect, not only on Tom, but on all his classmates and generations of students. Van Doren taught the "English Sequence," and his presentation of literature made it clear that literature was the very generator of spiritual life, that all philosophy depended on literature. His teaching was inflammatory, exciting even those students who became nauseated at the idea of opening a book. Mark Van Doren was not a follower of any camp; he was scornful of all camps and of all the camp-followers. He scoffed at left-wing pundits as second-rate minds and right-wing pundits as blockheads, and he wouldn't tolerate psychoanalyzing everybody from Homer to Shakespeare in terms of Freudian oedipuses.

Tom was fired up; this man really loved to teach! His students couldn't get away with feeding back what he gave them; he wanted to bring forth the ideas they didn't even know they had. He regarded them all as truth-seekers and therefore he imposed the disciplines of the truth-seeker on every one of his students. Nobody got by.

The other sequences in "Contemporary Civilization" were not all that enlightening, but in their own way they, too, brought to birth the truth that Tom was seeking. It was for one of the other sequences that Tom had to take a field trip one winter afternoon to visit Bellevue morgue. There he saw the rows and rows of iceboxes containing the blue, swollen corpses of people who had drowned, the dead who had been found frozen in the parks, huddled under piles of old newspapers, and the dead picked up in the streets—poisoned by the raw denatured alcohol the "bums" drank. The murdered were there, and the "dope fiends," taking their last trip, and those dead of venereal disease, and those killed by gangsters.

They had once been persons, born with their own uniquenesses which could never be duplicated, but no one would ever know what they had in them. They were waste—shipped daily up the East River on a barge to an island where New York's garbage was burned.

Tom thought somebody ought to do something about the waste and corruption in society, and many students thought as he did. The press, especially the Hearst newspapers, were at that time accusing Columbia of being a hotbed of Communism. The number of "Reds" was actually very small, but they made up for their lack of numbers with noise. They held meetings at the sundial on 116th Street. There Tom joined with the National Students League to protest the Italian invasion of Ethiopia. The big event of that spring of 1935 was the Peace Strike. Tom marched with the others, chanting: "Books, not battleships!" and "No more war!"

His enthusiasm for Communism lasted about three months. Then, at a party given in the Park Avenue apartment of a Barnard girl who belonged to the Young Communist League (her parents were away for the weekend), Tom discovered that the Young Communists didn't believe in getting drunk. They considered themselves disciplined members of a team. Such teamwork was too much for Tom, and he went out and bought whiskey and got drunk all by himself. That night a girl signed him up with the Young Communist League and, feeling cheerful, he took the name of Frank Swift. It was a prophetic name, for it certainly was the swift end of his Communist career. Shortly after this he dropped

out of the group. With a little whiskey in him he could take
the boredom of Communist harangues; sober, it was too
much. Also, he discovered that under the idealistic procla-
mations of brotherhood and justice, Communists were the
same selfish human beings as any bourgeois trying to climb
the status ladder.

That summer, Tom and his brother went swimming, listened to jazz records, and wandered around Douglaston,
bored. They had no car and walked the two or three miles to
Great Neck to go to the movies, sitting through all the stupid, vapid movies that were ever made, hating them but not
leaving.

At last, summer was over. Tom rushed off to Columbia
studying the catalogue of courses. His arms were full of new
notebooks just waiting to be filled, and he had a new suit and
a new hat.

John Paul was also off to a university that fall, but he went
to Cornell. Very soon it appeared that his first year at Cornell was going to be at least as disastrous as Tom's had been
at Cambridge, as if John Paul had to outdo his older brother.

Tom, having come through the dangerous undertow, had
discovered in himself a capacity for hard work—it just depended on what the work was.

On the fourth floor of John Jay Hall were the offices of the
student publications, the glee club, chess club, varsity show,
and student board. It was the noisiest, most intellectual part
of the campus. Tom approached the fourth floor cir-
cumspectly. First he went to his adviser and asked how to get
into things. His adviser gave him a letter of introduction to
the editor of the university literary magazine, *The Columbia
Review*.

Tom wrote for everything. He wrote stories for the daily
Spectator, assisted on the yearbook, and became art editor of
the *Jester*. He wrote reviews for the *New York Times*; he
wrote for commercial firms like Dixie Cup. He had a job as a
guide on the observation roof of the RCA building at Rocke-
feller Center. He worked in a publicity management office.
And he put his name in for the cross-country team. Accepted,

he helped make it the worst cross-country team in the East that year.

Along with all this, Tom carried eighteen units of courses, dated girls three or four nights a week, and went with his fraternity brothers to sit in a smoke-filled cellar nightclub. "It was a strange, animal travesty of mysticism, sitting in those booming rooms, with the noise pouring through you, and the rhythm . . . throbbing."

On such nights, he'd miss the train back to Douglaston and have to go home by subway and bus. Waiting in the dismal station at that gray hour before dawn, he glanced at those who waited with him—gray-faced youths, ashen in the bleak light, and drunken soldiers. They all looked like "the prototypes I had seen in the morgues . . . among all these I stood, weary and ready to fall, lighting the fortieth or fiftieth cigarette . . . the one that took the last shreds of lining off my throat."

Next day, back he would bounce. One of his college friends, Ed Rice, said Tom was the noisiest of all the noise-makers on the fourth floor. "Amid all the confusion on the fourth floor, I heard an incredible, noisy, barrel-house blues piano drowning out everything else . . . like four men playing at once. 'Who is the crowd playing the piano?' I asked. 'Only Merton,' was the answer."

That fall, Tom signed up for courses in economics, sociology, political science—all the areas he had been neglecting in favor of literature, poetry, and philosophy.

Climbing the crowded stairways of Hamilton Hall, he went into the room for the opening class of his history course and was surprised to see so many people he knew, fellows who worked on the *Jester* with him. It was odd that all these literary types, his cronies from the fourth floor, were taking this history course, too.

He put down his load of books; just then the professor entered, and Tom immediately realized he'd made a mistake. Mark Van Doren taught Shakespeare in this room. Confused, Tom gathered himself and his books together and started for the door; then suddenly, he turned and came back. It was the most important choice of his college career. At last he had entered his own element. He was where he belonged. Mark

Van Doren's classroom was a place where students discussed ideas. They spoke of literature, philosophy, and even the most taboo of all subjects, spiritual essences. No one dared pollute the intellectual atmosphere with platitudes, cant or labels coined by the Marxists, Freudians, or Darwinians. "All that year we were, in fact, talking about the deepest springs of human desire and hope and fear; we were considering all the most important realities."

Tom Merton became close friends with Bob Lax—a chap with a long face and a mane of black hair who was a poet and a nonconformist. Lax would go for hours without speaking, and people would think him inarticulate, but suddenly he would begin to talk, and once he began, he could talk nonstop. But he could not talk about trivia; he liked to talk about God. It was his quest for the Absolute that attracted Tom so strongly. Merton was a Celt and a Welshman, Lax a Jew and Old Testament man—both so different from each other, yet so alike in their quest for the God of Abraham, Isaac, Jacob, and St. John of the Cross.

One Sunday night, coming home late to Douglaston from a field trip to the Pennsylvania coal mines for his geology course, Tom felt icy November was in his bones. He crept stealthily upstairs and went to bed. Next morning, Tom looked into his grandfather's room on his way to school. Pop was sitting up in bed and he looked bad.

"How do you feel?" Tom asked.

"Rotten," said his grandfather.

Tom advised him to go back to sleep a bit longer and then dashed off to make his train. Late that afternoon, he was out on the track when one of the juniors came up and called to Tom: "Your aunt was on the phone just now. She said your grandfather is dead."

The train to Douglaston took forever, it seemed, but at last he arrived home. He went directly upstairs into his grandfather's room. Someone had opened the windows. The room was icy cold and Tom, knowing how Pop feared drafts and dreaded the least cold (he kept the house overheated), went to close the windows. Then he remembered it didn't make any difference. His grandfather, lying on the bed under the sheet, would not feel the drafts any more. He who had been alive this morning was dead.

Suddenly Tom did something he had never done before—he got down on his knees by the bed and began to pray for the soul of a dead person. It must have been the spontaneous response to his love for Pop—yet it was strange, because he had loved others who had died and he'd never had such an impulse. Only now it had come, the need and desire to pray for the dead.

He thought of Pop. Once, hanging onto a strap in the Seventh Avenue subway in New York, Tom found himself staring at a white card with a picture of red jellied soup, advertising "White Rose Jellied Consommé Madrilène." Vividly he recalled a scene with his godfather. They were having supper and his godfather glanced at the people next to them and predicted they would order consommé madrilène.

"Why?" asked Tom.

"People from the suburbs always order consommé madrilène as soon as they see it on the menu," his godfather assured him.

Tom was astonished and filled with admiration for his godfather when, as soon as the waiter came, he heard the people order: "Consommé madrilène!"

Pop would have ordered consommé madrilène. He had no "culture," he was not knowledgeable about gourmet foods, didn't know how to serve wines.

Merton later wrote, "The world of civilization and books, of ease and humor, of good conversation, art and music, of good restaurants . . . in London—and, of course on the Continent. The world of Cambridge colleges, and rowing, and rugger, and concerts, and audit ale in Hall, and tea at my Italian tutor's. . . ." That was "the complete world I believed in and lived in at Cambridge." It was a world that fostered Tom's innate gift for sarcasm. But at Columbia, Tom was learning a more compassionate humanism from Mark Van Doren. Judging people sarcastically could be your own loss.

Tom had grown closer to Pop during these Columbia years and argued with him less. Pop would often call Tom and ask him to come downtown for lunch. They'd meet and Pop would tell Tom his troubles and they would talk about Tom's future. Bit by bit Tom gained insight into this simple man and realized that Pop was not as naive as he had thought. More important, he was a kind, warm-hearted human being and underneath his booming American optimism was a perplexity, a sadness, and a questioning.

Bonnemaman had been tremendously attached to her husband. Now she began to fade, and month after month she seemed to get weaker, until by the following summer there could be no doubt she was dying. In August 1937, she died. For hours Tom stood beside her bed praying—he no longer questioned his need to pray. Later, he prayed for himself, too.

It happened like this. He was coming into the city on the Long Island train and suddenly he felt dizzy. He stood up, heading for the gap between the cars—he wanted air. But his knees began to shake. All he could do was prop himself against the wall and hold on until the train got in.

Immediately he made his way across the street to the Pennsylvania Hotel and asked for the house physician. The doctor said Tom was suffering from fatigue and should take a room, go to bed, and then return home the next day.

"I found myself in a room in the Pennsylvania Hotel, lying on a bed . . . and listened to the blood pounding rapidly inside my head. I could hardly keep my eyes closed. Yet I did not want to open them, either. I was afraid that if I even looked at the window, the strange spinning inside my head would begin again. That window! . . . far away in my mind was a little, dry, mocking voice that said: 'What if you threw yourself out of that window. . . .'"

Fragments of the past floated around him—the endless halls of Cambridge, the streets going nowhere, a rooming house in Bloomsbury, and the room where an Indian Ph.D. committed suicide. The doctor looked in on him again and ordered Tom to sleep, leaving some pills for that purpose. But the minute the doctor left, Tom decided to leave also and got up, went downstairs, paid for the room, and returned home.

In Douglaston, the doctor confirmed his need for rest and said he might possibly have an ulcer. Tom thought this meant he should eat nothing but ice cream, so for the rest of the year he ate quarts and quarts of ice cream, getting pudgy and falling in love with a girl who lived on his street. One evening he asked her out, but she said she was tired and wanted to stay home. Ten minutes later, she drove off with a rival. He went back to the house depressed and ate more ice cream.

The school year so energetically started came creaking to an end. With the close of the year came one last testimony to Tom's labors—the yearbook, full of pictures of Tom. After all, he was the editor.

He didn't graduate that June because he had entered Columbia in February. He still had a couple of courses to take.

One afternoon in November, Tom and Bob Lax were riding downtown on a bus. Bob was telling Tom about a new book by Aldous Huxley, *Ends and Means*. As the bus moved along Fifth Avenue, they saw Scribner's bookstore, and Tom said: "Let's go in to Scribner's and see if they have it."

They did. Tom bought the book and took it home with him and began to read. He could not put the book down. Excited and inspired, he was utterly absorbed. When he finished, he sat down and wrote a review-essay about it.

Huxley had been one of Tom's favorite novelists ever since Tom was sixteen and had first read Huxley's biting tales of the younger generation of upper-middle-class Britain. But this was a new Aldous Huxley, and the ideas he proposed in this book of nonfiction were spiritual. Huxley's insight into the mystics of the ages and the essential mysticism of Truth was different from generally understood occultism, and Tom immediately recognized that a spiritual dilemma was at the heart of his own dissatisfaction with life. Tom thought that this kind of mysticism was religious.

Others thought so too, and were upset by Aldous Huxley's *Ends and Means*, saying he was surely headed for the Catholic Church. To those who admired Huxley's grandfather, Thomas Huxley—the famous agnostic who made Darwin's work on evolution his cause to champion against nineteenth-century theology—there could be no worse fate.

But Aldous Huxley had no intention of becoming a Roman Catholic. His family had suffered one convert to the

"Romans"—traumatically. His maternal grandfather, Tom Arnold, was the skeleton in the family closet. Huxley's maternal grandmother blamed John Newman, whose conversion "to Rome" was the scandal of the nineteenth-century's enlightened generation, for her husband's defection. To the end of her life she wrote bitter letters to Cardinal Newman, and poor Newman kept trying to assure her that he had nothing to do with the conversion of Tom Arnold. Aldous Huxley was always to reveal this conflicting heritage when he wrote of spiritual things, but it was perhaps just for this reason—that his mysticism was churchless—that he reached Merton.

The spiritual propositions set forth by Huxley—that man couldn't use evil means to attain good ends, that violence would not attain kindness, and war would not attain peace—found deep resonance in Thomas Merton. Huxley wrote that man was immersed in material and animal urges which made him blind, crude, and greedy, and unless he asserted dominance of mind and will over this inferior element he would never be free. Unless the spirit were freed, people would be doomed to live as beasts, tearing each other apart.

But what was really new to Tom's way of thinking was Huxley's assertion that the way to learn dominance of mind and will was through prayer and asceticism. That almost turned him off. Tom had been taught by the most advanced thinkers of his age that asceticism was bad for mankind because to repress yourself was masochism, a perversion of nature.

Happily, Huxley didn't push the idea of physical asceticism. Instead, he spoke of spiritual asceticism, using the term "detachment," which he defined as a discipline that enabled a person to overcome the enslavement of the senses and the flesh by dominating them, rather than the reverse.

Tom read Huxley's book over and over. He knew enough about the mystics to be able to challenge Huxley's argument that Christianity was less spiritual than Buddhism. Early in that same year he'd entered a course in French Medieval Literature, wanting to find out more about the old churches of France which his father had taken him to so many times.

While taking this course, Tom had seen a book in Scribner's, *The Spirit of Medieval Philosophy* by Etienne

Gilson. He went in and bought it, then when he got home, he noticed for the first time the small print on page 1: "Nihil obstat. . . ." Angrily he threw the book down. Those words stood for Catholic censorship!

It took him a while to bring himself to look into the book, but when he did he became fascinated. Gilson gave Tom a definition for God such as he had never heard: God is Being Itself.

Astounded, Tom underlined the words. *God is Being Itself.* That was all. God existed by virtue of being God, not caused by any cause, and having no justification for being. He was Being Itself.

Gilson's concept of God was simple yet baffling: "When God says that He is Being . . . if what He says is to have any intelligible meaning to our minds, it can only mean this: that He is the pure act of existing." Tom underlined like mad. Up to this time he'd taken for granted the prevalent ideas about God, and accepted without question that Christians believed (as they often said) that their God was vindictive, moralistic, respectable, and had all the human vices except sex.

How different were Gilson's ideas! Tom had never heard such ideas, and suddenly he was aware that the everyday opinions about the nature of God were not only inadequate but stupid. Gilson and Huxley had stimulated the mystical hunger in Tom's soul and he yearned for a religious way to reach this God. He wanted to do more than read and intellectualize; he wanted to act, to do something.

Alone in the big living room at Douglaston, now so empty with Pop and Bonnemaman gone and John Paul away at Cornell, Tom sat for hours, reading about mystics. December 1937 turned into January 1938. Thomas Merton graduated from Columbia. No fanfare—he went up to the registrar's window and was handed his Bachelor of Arts diploma. He immediately went to another window and put his name down for more courses, in the Graduate School of English. The collapse of his health had made him think about his choice of career, and he decided that he didn't want to get into any more rat races.

"This registration in the graduate school represented the

first remote step of a retreat from the fight for money and fame, the active and worldly life of conflict and competition. If anything, I would now be a teacher and live the rest of my life in the relative peace of a college campus, reading and writing books." He chose an unknown novelist of the eighteenth century for his master's thesis.

Then one day, as he was walking past the wire fences by the tennis courts, his vision was transfixed by light. It was merely the light playing along the wires, but the light was poetry, the wires were like metal strings of a harpsichord, and on these metal strings the light played harmonies. Image became word, word became person, and suddenly Tom knew what the musical harmonies were playing—they were playing William Blake. He changed the subject of his master's thesis to Blake.

"Oh, what a thing it was to live in contact with the genius and holiness of William Blake that year, that summer, writing the thesis!"

That June, Tom moved out of the Douglaston house. He got in a taxi with his bags, books, portable victrola, records, pictures, and tennis racket, and moved to a rooming house on 114th Street, behind Columbia's library.

It was a Hindu monk who made Tom read the Christian mystics. The monk's name was Bramachari. His picture had been tacked on the door of the room where Bob Lax and Sy Freedgood lived when Tom first arrived at Columbia. Bramachari had come to America from his ashram in India to represent his monastery at the World Congress of Religions held in Chicago in 1932. He was given scarcely enough money for his ticket. It didn't last all the way, and so he was a long time getting to America. By the time he arrived, the World Congress of Religions was over and the buildings were being demolished. Various religious groups invited him to give lectures and people lent or gave him money. By the time Tom met Bramachari, the Hindu monk had been in America several years and had acquired a Ph.D. from the University of Chicago.

Tom never forgot the first time he saw the shy little man with the yellow turban. Bramachari immediately encouraged

Merton's spirituality. He advised him to turn to the Christian teachings of St. Augustine, assuring Tom that there was a tremendous mystical tradition in Christianity. The more Tom immersed himself in the Christian mystics and in the works of William Blake, the more he became fascinated by the Catholic Mass.

One Sunday he telephoned the girl he was seeing and told her he wouldn't be out to Long Island that weekend. Tom had decided to go to Mass. Although he'd been in a thousand Catholic churches, he'd never heard the Mass, because if he happened to chance on a Mass, he fled.

"This was one of the few things I got from Pop that really took root in my mind, and became part of my mental attitude: this hatred and suspicion of Catholics." To Pop the Church was a sinister bunch that had persecuted his own Masonic order. Popes were bad medicine and the Mass was bad magic.

It was a rare Sunday, the first time Tom woke up really sober on a Sunday morning in New York. He walked to Mass along empty streets. The church was a small brick church, Corpus Christi, behind Teachers' College on 121st Street.

Tom was surprised to see how full it was, and how ordinary everybody looked, young people with families and old people, every color and class of humanity. All these ordinary-looking people were engaging in strange rites, like striking their breasts, kneeling, admitting they were sinners, praying. It was mysterious. Then small bells began to ring and people moved from every corner of the church into the aisle, and followed one another slowly, in line, to the rail at the altar.

Tom got scared. He genuflected and hurried out of the church. He walked down Broadway in a daze. Everything was lit up. New York was shining. Light was everywhere.

7

I am about to make my home/In the bell's summit . . .

The books piled higher and higher on Tom's desk. He was in the middle of his thesis on *Nature and Art in William Blake*. It was a study of Blake's reaction against naturalism and narrow realism, because the poet's own ideal was essentially mystical and supernatural.

The kind of love which Blake glorified was the transfiguration of man's natural love in the fires of mystical experience. That implied purification, Tom realized. Blake had a moral insight that cut through the norms of pride, greed, and lust.

By the time Merton was ready to begin the actual writing of his thesis it was September 1938. On one of those hot evenings at the end of summer, Tom had left his desk and gone out for a walk. It was a pleasant, soporific evening after the sultry day, when suddenly the quiet murmurs of radios coming through open windows merged into a big, ominous voice.

Tom heard: "Germany . . . Hitler . . . at six o'clock this morning the German Army . . . the Nazis. . . ." The Germans had occupied Czechoslovakia.

He went back to his room. A friend came in and they sat

until after midnight, drinking beer, smoking, making excited jokes about the coming war with a sort of graveyard humor.

A couple of days later, the English prime minister flew to see Hitler and they made a new alliance at Munich. The prime minister came back reassuring everyone of "peace in our time." The Nazis had only been testing out their blitzkrieg strategy once more. Last year Spain, this year Czechoslovakia. True, the Nazis now occupied Czechoslovakia, but what could anyone do? Not that people didn't care. They cared. They had cared about Spain, too. But in the meantime, while there was "peace in our time," people went back to their own personal preoccupations.

One rainy day, Tom had been working in the library. As he walked back to his room, looking at the rain as it fell gently on the empty tennis courts across the street, he reminded himself that he had to give a tutoring lesson later that afternoon.

Inside, he sat down to read a book he'd borrowed on the life of the English poet Gerard Manley Hopkins. The chapter told of Hopkins' thinking of becoming a Catholic and writing a letter to Cardinal Newman (not then a cardinal).

The rain was streaming on the windowpanes, and suddenly Tom felt, rather than heard, a voice saying: "What are you waiting for, Tom? Why don't you do it?"

He stood up and walked restlessly about the room. "It's absurd," he thought. But even while he was trying to talk himself out of it, he was putting on his raincoat.

Outside, he walked along the gray wooden fence toward Broadway. The chilling rain was good. He turned his face up to it. He walked the nine blocks to 121st Street, turned the corner, went up to the brick church, over to the door of the rectory, and rang the bell. When the door opened he said:

"May I see Father Ford, please?"

Father Ford was out. Tom turned away and started down the street. There was Father Ford coming around the corner from Broadway. Tom went to meet him and said:

"Father, may I speak to you about something?"

"Yes, sure, come into the house." They went in.

"Father, I want to become a Catholic."

The priest nodded and gave Tom three books. "Read these, think about them, then come back."

In a way, it was like the three tasks always demanded of heroes in fairy tales, the three obstacles they have to overcome before being permitted to marry the fair maiden.

Soon Thomas Merton was taking instruction in the faith of the Catholic Church. The more he learned, the more he "began to burn with the desire for baptism."

Bob Lax and Bob Gerdy talked constantly about their course on the Catholic philosophers and Tom realized how little he knew about them, especially Thomas Aquinas and Duns Scotus. He decided to take the course, and went to see Professor Dan Walsh. Walsh had the rare ability to see the wholeness of Catholic philosophy, beyond the different schools of thought.

As November began, Tom's mind was centered on getting baptized. He felt that he was about to set foot on the shore, at the bottom of the "seven-circled mountain of a Purgatory steeper and more arduous than I was able to imagine." He was anxious to begin the climb.

The date was set for the sixteenth of November. As the time got close, Tom began to get nervous. On the night of the fifteenth, he lay in bed awake, consumed with fear. All kinds of worries occurred to him. He might not remember what to do. Things might go wrong and humiliate him. He couldn't sleep. What if he couldn't keep the eucharistic fast?

Those were the days when a Catholic had to refrain from eating or drinking from midnight to whatever Mass he or she was going to attend. Later Pope John XXIII compassionately shortened the fast required for taking communion at Mass to just one hour.

As Tom thought about fasting from food and water until ten o'clock the next morning, he got thirstier and thirstier. If he could just take a drink, one sip. His throat felt parched and he feared it was going to be beyond his strength to lie in bed and not get up for a drink of water.

Somehow he held out. At last, morning came. Now he had another worry. What if he should accidentally on purpose swallow just a tiny bit of water while washing his teeth? He decided not to wash his teeth. He started to light a cigarette.

One more problem! Could you or couldn't you smoke before taking communion? He solved that one by putting the cigarette back in the pack.

And now he was going down the stairs, he was out in the street, he was walking to the church—a man going to his execution, "my happy execution and rebirth." The weather was frosty and above him the bright cold sky glittered like a steel sword, the city wore plumes of smoke upon helmets of ice. There were his good friends, they were going to stand by him: Ed Rice, the only Catholic among them, was to be his godfather; the others, Bob Lax, Seymour Freedgood, and Bob Gerdy, were Jews. Quietly they went into the church.

It was all very simple. First Tom knelt at the altar of Our Lady and abjured all heresy; then they went to the baptistry, in a little dark corner. Tom was praying:

"Incline to my aid, O God—O Lord, make haste to help me."

The priest was asking him his name. What do you want of the Church? he demanded. Tom replied that he wanted to believe. Faith. He said it in Latin: *"Fidem!"* It was all in Latin.

The priest asked him faith in what, and Tom said: "Life everlasting, *Vitam aeternam.*"

The priest now began the exorcism of Thomas Merton.

"Do you renounce Satan and all his works?"

Tom was thinking of his greedy ambitions, the lust for fame, the drive for selfish fulfillments. He said: "I do renounce Satan and his works. I do renounce them."

The priest breathed three times into Tom's face and said: *"Exi ab eo, spiritus immunde."* Go out of him, unclean spirit, and make room for the Holy Spirit.

Tom felt a great wind of spiritual cleansing go through him. It frightened the devils right out of him, "the legion that had been living in me for twenty-three years . . . I did not see them leaving, but there must have been more than seven of them. I had never been able to count them."

He was elated. "I have found the fountains of the spring where the Lord refreshes the morning. He has laid his hand on my shoulder."

And meanwhile the priest was saying: "Thomas, receive

the good Spirit through this breathing, receive the blessing of God, peace be with thee," and he signed Tom with crosses and then put salt upon his tongue to keep him forever fresh and savory, because salt keeps meat from rotting. "If thou be not already baptized," said the priest, "I baptize thee, Thomas, in the name of the Father, the Son, and the Holy Ghost." He poured the water on Tom's head.

Then Tom went to confession. Kneeling in the shadows, he hoped the priest was not too young to be told all the things he was going to confess to him. At last it was over and he "came stumbling out" and knelt at the front of the church.

The little bells rang, but Tom didn't get up frightened and run out of the church, as heretofore, because this was *his* Mass. He had been shriven—forgiven—and belonged where he was. The little bells rang their silver notes, the candles burned, and the priest came to Tom and gave him the small piece of white unleavened bread, the Host.

"My First Communion began to come towards me, down the steps, I was the only one at the altar rail . . . this solitariness was a kind of reminder of the singleness with which this Christ, hidden in the small Host, was giving himself to me."

Alone. The theme of his life was in this moment. The theme was that he was to climb the mountain of God as a mystic, which means one who goes alone to meet the Lord.

The friends who had come to stand by him, shoulder to shoulder, were welcoming him back to their pew. They knelt with him after communion.

The priest invited everyone to the rectory for breakfast, and they ate hungrily, laughing, everybody talking. After it was over, they went outside and didn't know where to go.

"It was after eleven o'clock and nearly time for lunch and we had just had breakfast. How could we have lunch? And if, at twelve o'clock, we did not have lunch, what was there for us to do?"

Suffering a great letdown after the spiritual high of the morning, Tom and his friends ambled down the street. What shall we do now? Where shall we go? Was this all religion was? Merely the ringing of a bell? Not getting the answers?

New Year's Day, 1939. At the end of the month Tom would be twenty-four, and he still didn't know what he wanted to be. He took his exams for the M.A. and then went to Bermuda to see again childhood places where he'd gone with his father. He returned within a week, just in time to say good-by to Bramachari, who was going back to India. Tom thought of the lesson in prayer discipline that Bramachari had given him on New Year's Day. While everybody else was suffering from hangovers, Bramachari had got up at the crack of dawn to chant his prayers.

After seeing him off, Tom went to Greenwich Village and signed a lease on an apartment on Perry Street. There he settled to work on his Ph.D. thesis which was on Gerard Manley Hopkins.

The apartment on Perry Street was one large room with a fireplace and French windows leading onto a rickety balcony. There Tom could sit and be inspired. He worked not only on his thesis, but he also wrote poetry.

"How many envelopes I fed to the green mailbox at the corner of Perry Street just before you got to Seventh Avenue! And everything I put in there came back—except for the book reviews."

One night in spring, he and Bob Lax were walking down Sixth Avenue. The street was torn up, trenched and banked with dirt, and marked with red lanterns where the city was digging the subway. Bob suddenly asked: "What do you want to be, anyway?"

What did he want to be? The writer of all those book reviews in the back pages of newspapers, or Thomas Merton, professor of freshman English? He blurted out: "I guess I want to be a good Catholic."

Bob Lax shook his head. "What you should say is that you want to be a saint."

"I can't be a saint," he said, humorous but also irritated.

Lax replied: "All that is necessary to be a saint is to want to be one."

The next day Tom told Mark Van Doren: "Lax is going around saying all a man needs to be a saint is to want to be one."

"Of course," said Mark.

It was easy for them to talk, they weren't the ones being pushed—Tom was. He was the one who was burning for God. He sat in his room on Perry Street and read St. John of the Cross, underlining heavily. Then he threw his pencil down. It would take more than underlining St. John of the Cross to make him a saint.

Summer came. Bob Lax's brother-in-law had a summer cottage in Olean, on the Allegheny River. Tom Merton and Ed Rice and Bob Lax moved in with their typewriters and all immediately began writing novels. At St. Bonaventure College, just a few miles away, they could borrow books from the library. The librarian, Father Irenaeus, not only gave them the use of the college library, he gave them the freedom of his own library.

Such kindly influences inspired them to write recklessly. Ed Rice finished his novel in ten days, 150 pages long and illustrated. Bob Lax wrote several novels, that is, he wrote several fragments of novels which he put together. Only Tom wrote on and on, his novel getting longer and longer, until at last it was five hundred pages. He decided to rewrite it, make it shorter. Then he changed the title again; this was the third title change.

By the middle of August, when they returned to New York, Tom was ready to begin sending his novel around to publishers. Later, in *The Secular Journal*, Merton tells the woes of the young writer:

"This time last year *The Labyrinth* had just been rejected by Macmillan. Since then it has been to Viking, Knopf, Harcourt Brace, then to the agent Curtis Brown, who sent it to Modern Age, Atlantic Monthly Books, McBride, and now Carrick and Evans. . . . So many bad books get printed, why can't *my* bad book get printed?"

The fall of 1939 was an ominous time. The world waited in suspense, sick with fascinated helplessness, for the Nazi war machine to strike. During the first week in September, Tom woke one morning to hear the scream of radios. At first he couldn't make out what had happened, then he understood—the Nazis were bombing Warsaw.

He went to early Mass, knelt by the altar rail and prayed.

This is it, he thought, the Second World War is beginning and "we all share in the responsibility. . . . Hitler is not the only one. . . . I have my share in it . . . the sins of the whole selfish world. . . ."

One night, Tom and Ed Rice and a group of friends sat in a bar until four in the morning, and then all went to Tom's apartment to bed down wherever they could. It was not unusual for Tom to sleep on the floor or on a couch too narrow and too short, when everybody got together for a party. To make yourself this uncomfortable just for fun seemed idiotic. Yet if anyone had suggested he sleep so uncomfortably for spiritual reasons, he would have said they were sappy.

Later, when they got up and were playing Beiderbecke records and looking stupefied, Tom suddenly said: "I am going to be a priest."

They just looked at him. It didn't make sense. But after everyone went home, Tom went to the campus to find Dan Walsh. Walsh was not in his office, so Tom went to a phone booth and called him. He told Tom that he had a dinner engagement but they could meet downtown later that night.

Sitting in a far corner of the Biltmore bar, Tom told Dan Walsh he was thinking about the priesthood. Walsh said:

"You know, the first time I met you I thought you had a vocation to the priesthood."

Tom said he'd heard a lot of things about monasteries. They fasted too much, monastic obedience was too heavy, and they prayed at all hours, especially at night. His health might crack up and then what? They'd throw him back into the world, a hopeless moral and physical wreck.

Dan Walsh began talking about a retreat he had made the summer before at a Trappist monastery in Kentucky called Our Lady of Gethsemani. He spoke at length about the solitude, the silence of the monks, so that Tom got the impression the monks never spoke. "Don't they even go to confession?" he asked.

Walsh then explained that of course they did and they also talked to their abbot, to guests, and sang in choir.

"I suppose they fast a lot," Tom muttered.

"They fast more than half the year," Dan assured him, "and they never eat meat or fish unless they get sick. They don't even have eggs, but live on vegetables, cheeses and things like that."

Merton could see it all—the monastery, a gray prison with barred windows through which one could see the emaciated monks, their hoods pulled down over their faces.

"They are very healthy," said Dan. "Big strong men."

Tom sat in silence, possessed by a strange feeling of mingled fear and exhilaration. But when Dan Walsh asked: "Do you think you'd like that life?" Tom cried: "No way. It would kill me in a week. I have to have meat. I need it for my health."

At the end of their talk, Walsh gave Merton a note to Father Edmund at the monastery of St. Francis of Assisi on 31st Street. There Tom went to seek his vocation. Father Edmund asked him about his family background, and then said Tom could probably enter the novitiate next February.

"Do you have enough to live on?" Father Edmund asked.

"I've got a chance of a job teaching English in extension at Columbia this year, and besides that they gave me a grant-in-aid to pay for my courses for the doctorate."

"Good, get busy on that doctorate . . . you'll probably end up teaching at St. Bona's."

Elated, Thomas Merton went away and began going to church for Mass every morning and returning every afternoon to make the Stations of the Cross. Sometimes he was exhausted after a long day of lectures and study, he could hardly concentrate on the fourteen stations, but he felt making the effort was what counted.

As winter turned to spring, Tom's body rebelled. He got an agonizing stomach ache. It was appendicitis and he had to go into the hospital for surgery.

Carrying Dante's *Paradiso*, in Italian, under his arm, plus Maritain's *Preface to Metaphysics*, Thomas Merton entered St. Elizabeth Hospital and was led peacefully away by a Franciscan nun to be made ready for surgery.

From the hospital he went home to Douglaston to recuperate. There he began writing meditations which were really scathing criticisms of the Church's reluctance to take social actions, especially for racial justice. He cited examples of Catholic parochial schools that argued against admitting black children by saying it was not "prudent." Merton said they were like Judas. Judas also fell back on prudence. That is, he looked first at the money box when the woman poured all the ointment on Christ's body. Judas explained that she was wasting precious ointment that could have been sold and the money given to the poor. Tom barely had turned Catholic and already he was ringing the alarm bell to wake up people.

By the middle of Easter week, the doctor said that Tom had recuperated sufficiently to go on a brief vacation. He decided to go to Cuba, calling his journey a medieval pilgrimage. That is, he explained, nine-tenths vacation and one-tenth holy. His experiences in a Catholic country, full of churches, convinced him that he belonged in the Church, body and soul.

He wrote: "Here in niches were those lovely, dressed up images, those little carved Virgins full of miracle and pathos and clad in silks and black velvet . . . Here, in side chapels, were those pietàs fraught with fierce Spanish drama, with thorns and nails whose very sight pierced the mind and heart . . ." while outside, even during Mass, the hoarse shouts of the sellers of lottery tickets could be heard. He wrote a poem about the girls of Cuba—the white girls and the black girls. At the end of the poem they all fly away like birds, probably because this was what was going to happen as soon as Tom entered the monastery.

Back in New York at the end of May, he went to the monastery on 31st Street, and Father Edmund told him his application had been accepted. All was in readiness for Thomas Merton to enter the novitiate the coming fall.

Before going to Olean that summer, he took a trip to Ithaca to see John Paul at Cornell. His brother responded warmly to Tom's new faith and even went to Mass every morning with Tom. He told Tom he had got acquainted with the Catholic chaplain at Cornell and they had a lot in common—they both liked flying planes.

Underneath this easy congeniality, Tom recognized the uneasy restlessness that had marked his own spiritual boredom and emptiness at Cambridge. All day long John Paul would drive up and down the valley in his big secondhand Buick, wandering from place to place through all the little towns.

After the brothers had visited together for a few days, Tom went on upstate to Olean, but soon discovered that the summer cottage was overcrowded. Also, hitchhiking the few miles to St. Bonaventure's for Mass every morning took too long, so Tom asked if there was a place he could live at St. Bonaventure's. The monastery on the college campus was filled with clerics from the different houses of studies, registered for the summer session. But Tom was permitted to share the dilapidated room in the gymnasium that was occupied by three or four poor students and some seminarians.

He entered into the Franciscan life ardently, getting up when the clerics did, going to early Mass and communion, and then to breakfast. Afterward he would walk to the library. In the afternoons he would pray the divine office in the woods, or walk along the Allegheny River. Already he saw himself in brown robe and sandals.

During this summer, he continually received letters from the novice-master, with printed lists of things Tom was to bring with him to the monastery. It was almost like going to a new school, and he felt the same tense excitement, pleasurable but nerve-racking.

Then one night he awoke from a restless sleep, a feeling of indescribable anguish in his soul. Suddenly he felt the whole thing was impossible. He had been an idiot to think he dare attempt the priesthood. He was a sinner.

"I have to go and let Father Edmund know."

He packed a bag and took the train to New York. The train seemed the slowest train anybody ever took, crawling through the green valleys, taking all the time in the world. Peering out of the window, Tom saw a boy running up a path toward his mother who stood on a porch, calling. He felt an ache, as if from an old wound, the ache of his own homelessness.

Father Edmund listened as Tom poured out the story of his life and his troubled past. Tom was hoping perhaps he wouldn't take it all that seriously. Maybe he would just say: "What's past is past, forget it, you're starting a new life."

He didn't. Father Edmund looked very serious and told

Tom he'd pray over the matter and let Tom know in a couple of days. Tom was appalled. How could he wait that long? Compassionately, Father Edmund relented. "Come back tomorrow."

The next day, Father Edmund told Thomas Merton he should write the Provincial and tell him he had reconsidered his application.

Stunned, Tom walked away from the monastery. He went into a church and saw the light on over the confessional that meant a priest was hearing confessions. He entered the confessional and poured out his heart, weeping, overcome with bewilderment. The priest, hearing his tearful, mixed-up confession, got irritated. He told Tom that anybody as emotional and unstable as Tom definitely did not belong in a monastery, least of all in the priesthood. A man had to be strong, an athlete of the soul, to be a priest, and he didn't want Tom wasting any more of his time coming into the confessional to indulge in self-pity.

Somehow Tom got to his feet and made it out of the confessional. He was completely broken. He covered his face with his hands, but the tears ran down between his fingers.

As the days passed, he slowly recovered his composure, and even a certain peace. He realized he could be a spiritual man, even a Christian mystic, without being in a monastery. So he put on his best blue suit and returned to St. Bonaventure to apply for a job as an English teacher. Gladly they gave him the job, and by the second week in September he was living in a small room on the second floor of the big red brick building that was both dormitory and monastery, with his books, typewriter, and the old portable phonograph he'd been dragging from place to place ever since Oakham.

His classes were composed of big boys from the mining and oil towns of Pennsylvania, football players and seminarians.

"I think they would enjoy Beowulf after I point out its close similarity to football. Wait until they try to figure out Chaucer, I'll need a bodyguard for the Chaucer lessons," he wrote.

All that winter, while Tom was teaching about the England of Chaucer and Shakespeare, Britain was being bombed.

Every morning he would go to the library and read the head-lines about places he had known, destroyed by the saturation bombing. In his diary he wrote about war and what it meant to take up the cause of peace, trying to think it through.

"If I pray for peace, that prayer is only justified if it means one thing"—it had to mean that he himself could sacrifice affluence, the things that make for greed. Just praying for a cessation of war wasn't enough. Merton quoted Léon Bloy. Bloy had described the human race as a tree, and if the tree bore bad fruit, if the tree bore murderers, well that meant that murderers were the fruit of all the people. "That applies to Hitler," wrote Merton. "We are a tree of which he is one of the fruits, and we all nourish him."

On an icy, bright January day Thomas Merton turned twenty-six and entered the momentous year of his life.

". . . the idea came to me that I might make a retreat in some monastery for Holy Week and Easter . . . the first place that came into my mind was the Trappist abbey Dan Walsh had told me about. . . ."

At the beginning of March he wrote the Trappists and soon received a reply saying they'd be glad to have him. At the same time a letter came from his draft board. His num-ber was up for service.

Tom had thought out his position on the war. He filled out his papers, requesting conscientious objector status. He said he would willingly serve in the medical corps, or as a stretcher bearer, or a hospital orderly. But he would not carry a gun.

Reporting for his physical examination, he climbed the an-cient stairs to the top floor of the Olean City Hall, tried the handle of the room marked Medical Board, and when the door opened, went in. He was too early. The doctor said, "We might as well begin. The others will be along in a minute."

Afterward, he wrote in his diary: "It was cold standing around in your skin passing from doctor to doctor." They looked at his teeth and were incredulous: "You certainly had a lot of teeth out!" They called everybody over to look in his mouth. Then the doctor told Tom he'd probably be classified

1-B, not 1-A, because so many of his teeth were out. They sent him on his way.

He went to the library and looked up the Trappists in the Catholic Encyclopedia and found they were also called Cistercians. The encyclopedia only gave him the basic facts, but for the moment it was the facts that interested him. The monastic order was founded at Cîteaux, in Burgundy, by Robert, Abbot of Molesme, in 1098. The Cistercian order combined the Benedictine rule for Christian monastic life with a life of agricultural work.

The Trappists were a branch of the Cistercians. The name Trappist came from the first abbey, La Trappe, founded at Soligny la Trappe (Orne, France) in 1140 by Rotron, Count de Perche. Trappists were noted for the extreme austerity of their rules, which included perpetual silence except in cases of strict necessity. They took five vows at the time of their profession: poverty, chastity, obedience, stability, and conversion of manners. One of the most significant vows was the vow of stability. This meant that a monk was bound to one monastic community unless his superiors decided to send him to help found a sister house. This vow of stability particularly fixed Tom's attention. After all his wanderings, he was fascinated by the idea of being bound to stay in one place for the rest of his life. At once the old fever for a religious order began to burn. No! he told himself. You have no vocation!

The Saturday before Palm Sunday, Tom was up at five A.M. He heard part of a Mass in the dark chapel, then ran through the rain to catch his train. He was on his way, riding through hills black in the dark wet weather, riding through valleys drenched in rain, riding through towns still asleep, going through Ohio.

In Cincinnati, he stayed over, and next morning took the train to Louisville. He waited in Louisville all day to take the train out to Gethsemani. At Bardstown Junction he stepped down out of the train into the empty night. There was a car standing there, and presently a man came out of a house and hurried to Tom. They got in the car and started up the road in the midst of moonlit fields.

"Are the monks in bed?" he asked the driver.

"Oh, yes, they go to bed at seven o'clock."

The pale ribbon of road stretched ahead of them, and then suddenly he saw a steeple, shining in the moonlight, behind a rounded knoll.

8

Slowly slowly/Comes Christ through the ruins
Seeking the lost disciple/A timid one/Too literate
To believe words/so he hides

The Abbey of Our Lady of Gethsemani was situated in a wide valley of rolling land, woods, cedars, and green fields. From the guesthouse, Tom could see the monastery barns and the vineyard which were nearby. Outside the windows apple trees were in blossom, and when he walked along the wall of the guesthouse garden, he saw tulips. The Trappist brothers in their medieval hoods and heavy, homemade boots would tramp along in a line through the vineyard. During that Easter week, Tom watched them at both work and prayer. On Holy Thursday when he went inside the cloister, the monks were washing the feet of some poor men, putting money in their hands, kissing their hands and feet, and giving them dinner. Bells rang in the steeple.

His Holy Week retreat at Gethsemani that Easter rang a bell in Thomas Merton. Tom heard the spiritual call always as the ringing of a bell. His baptism had been the ringing of an alarm clock, waking him up. The retreat at Gethsemani was a clearer, higher note, more like the ringing of a church bell. Years later, when he came to know the great Zen

Buddhist, Daisetz Suzuki, Thomas Merton spoke with him of the bell that awakens the soul. Suzuki nodded.

"Zen teaches nothing," he said, "it merely enables us to wake up and become aware. It does not teach. It points."

"Yes," agreed Merton vigorously, "the acts and gestures of a Zen Master are no more 'statements' than is the ringing of an alarm clock."

But part of Tom was still dozing. His longing for the monk's vocation was like a great void that had opened up in his solar plexus. He tried to fill it with everything else, since he was so sure that he had no vocation to the priesthood.

Back at St. Bona's, spring moved toward summer. In early June, Tom was busy giving exams, writing a new novel, and praying, according to "a Rule."

He was writing his new novel, *My Argument With the Gestapo*, in an experimental style, influenced by Franz Kafka and by James Joyce, and creating his own language, called "macaronic"—partly French, partly Italian, partly Spanish, partly English—yet understandable and very funny. It was an imaginary journey to the London of the saturation bombings. His humor was sardonic as he portrayed the self-discipline and asceticism often required by violence and war. He wrote: "There is, I think, going to be a crazy and half-hearted striving after self-discipline and unsystematic asceticism everywhere. It is going to look very funny indeed, in some of the violent maniacs that will associate it with various murders and other completely fantastic crimes! Anybody who really does want to deny himself is going to be put to great embarrassment by the numbers of ascetical murderers and self-denying dope fiends that are going to fill the world!"

What triggered Merton's sense of the absurd was a newspaper story about Rudolf Hess, one of Hitler's high officers. Taking off in a fighter plane to land on the estate of a friend in Glasgow, Scotland, Hess had the idea he could bring Britain "to its senses" and persuade her to come over to the side of the Nazis before England was bombed to fragments.

Even though German planes were at that moment dropping bombs on them, Hess's British friends politely invited him in for tea!

"I guess when the Germans invade England, someone will

run inland shouting, 'Visitors, unwelcome, but nevertheless, visitors,' and start making tea," wrote Merton. What really killed him, however, was Hess's superb response—he "never drank tea that late," he explained apologetically. Tom decided, humorously, that Hess probably refused the tea because he was afraid it would keep him awake.

What touched off Tom's sarcasm was the prophetic vision of self-denial for the sake of health. This was absurd, perverted morality, stemming from Rudolf Hess's vegetarian, nonsmoker, teetotaler asceticism—building up his own health with stern self-righteousness while in the very act of trying to destroy much of the rest of his own species.

"I feel good myself since I don't smoke or drink," wrote Tom, "but I don't understand people who give up these things just in order to feel good, or just because they think they are immoral. I only understand a man who likes smoking and drinking and doesn't think they are immoral and gives them up because he wants to give them up."

The idea of giving up everything had been much on Tom's mind. A year earlier, he had written about the war:

"The knowledge of what is going on . . . makes it seem desperately important to be voluntarily poor, to get rid of all possessions this instant. I am scared, sometimes, to own anything, even a name, let alone coin, or shares in the oil, munitions, the airplane factories. I am scared to take a proprietary interest in anything, for fear that my love of what I own may be killing somebody somewhere."

He saw what few saw at that time—that Christianity had arrived at a point where its validity had to be tested for those who called themselves Christians. The ground for the test was "priorities"—what came first for Christians, property or persons? Was property more sacred than lives? Greed stronger than love? For himself, the decision had to be to give up everything rather than let any possession or claim be a cause for killing somebody somewhere.

Writing his novel, Thomas Merton was, consciously or subconsciously, getting ready for great spiritual changes in his life. The novel was a stripping, an uncovering of layers of memory. He had to go through all the streets he had ever walked in order to work his way out of their maze. He said he would keep writing, putting things down until they became clear; at the same time, he admitted that even if they became clear, he wouldn't understand them.

My Argument With the Gestapo searched out all the places Thomas Merton had experienced in the building up of his identity.

"I came into this world because of Paris, since my father and mother met there as art students. . . .

"It is important to me that I have walked the dusty road under the plane trees from St. Antonin. . . ." There were times when he was mortally homesick for the south of France where he was born.

English angels went into the novel also, and bells.

"The quarterboys of Rye never cease to ring in my ears. I have known the silence of the marsh between Rye and Winchelsea. . . . Silence out toward Norwich and Lady Julian . . . Angels of the English west: of Exeter . . . the completely dark and empty church at St. Mary Redcliffe . . . Angels of Oxford . . . Angels of Cambridge . . . the bell in the tower of St. John's striking by night, heard in my digs in Bridge Street . . . Miss Maud's house near the village. . . . And Ripley. . . ."

He must keep alive in himself what he had once known and grown into—he was a writer. He must put it all down and pass it along.

On a humid night in August, the Baroness de Hueck came to speak at St. Bonaventure. Tom didn't feel like hearing a speaker, but when he stepped into the lecture hall, he stayed, fascinated. She was talking of her work in Harlem and was saying that Catholics had their nerve worrying about Communism when they were not living up to their obligations as Christians. They ought to worry about being Christians, she declared, and if they did that, they wouldn't have to worry about Communists.

"Come see Harlem," she called. "Come see Harlem with the eyes of Christ. The suffering of Christ is going on every instant in Harlem. Catholics, come see Harlem as a test of your love of Christ, as a test of your Christianity. Come see Negroes dying, being refused admission to a hospital. Come see Negroes evicted, jobless, no way to pay rent because no way to get a job."

This plain logic of Catherine de Hueck Doherty, foundress of Friendship House and of Madonna House, was the distillation of her years of meditation. As a young girl, the Baroness had escaped from her homeland at the time of the 1917 Russian Revolution. She ended up in New York, penniless, and got a job in a laundry. Her experiences of suffering and injustice had not destroyed her faith; in fact, it was just the opposite. More inflamed with God than ever, she was like a peaceful image in the midst of the fire.

When Tom learned that she was a member of the Third Order of St. Francis, he became more excited about her than ever, because he, too, wore the scapular of the Third Order of St. Francis under his shirt. Once again, he was aware that he could live in Christ, not as monk or priest, but as a man living in the world.

So next day he said to the baroness: "Would it be all right if I came to Friendship House and did a little work with you there?"

"Sure, come on," she said.

Only a short time later, in the middle of sweltering August, Thomas Merton entered Harlem. He came out of the subway and walked along the street until he arrived at stores marked Friendship House.

The ragged kids running through the dark warrens of the tenements, flying their kites on the roofs, mothers crying: "Don't fly your kite on the roof! Don't go up there, it will drag you away" became a poem in which Thomas Merton captured the terrible intensities of cruel, involuntary poverty; the poverty of the helpless poor:

"Across the cages of the keyless aviaries,/The lines and wires, the gallows of the broken kites,/Crucify, against the fearful light,/The ragged dresses of the little children./Soon, in the sterile jungles of the waterpipes and ladders,/The bleeding sun, a bird of prey, will terrify the poor."

He never forgot the huge, dark, steaming slum he was given to experience that August, where black people were crowded inhumanly, not free to move into other streets.

"In this huge cauldron, inestimable natural gifts, wisdom,

love, music, science, poetry are stamped down . . . souls are
destroyed by vice and misery and degradation, obliterated,
wiped out, washed from the register of the living, dehuman-
ized. What has not been devoured, in your dark furnace,
Harlem, by marijuana, by gin, by insanity, hysteria, syphilis?"

With amazing foresight, he predicted what the white-
majority society was to discover with chagrin a quarter-cen-
tury later—that black people saw the culture of white men as
spurious, fake, not worth the dirt in Harlem's gutters!

Years later, reading James Baldwin, Thomas Merton was
moved to write a letter to this fellow-writer who expressed
more passionately what he had said. "I am glad I am not a
Negro," he told Baldwin, "because I probably would never be
able to take it: but . . . I recognize in conscience that I have
a duty to try to make my fellow whites stop doing things they
do. . . ."

Tom stayed in Harlem working at Friendship House until
the end of August. He had promised himself a second
Trappist retreat before returning to his teaching post at St.
Bonaventure. Instead, he went to another monastery, in
Rhode Island, called Our Lady of the Valley.

He experienced no heightened states of prayer comparable
to the Holy Week retreat at Gethsemani, but he had time to
sort out the choices open to him. He could stay in the world
and write and teach. Or, he could go to Friendship House
and work in Harlem. Or he could become a Trappist. But his
mind refused to linger on this option.

The new teaching semester at St. Bonaventure's began,
and with it Tom embarked on a truly concentrated prayer
life. He got up before dawn each day to pray the "Little
Hours," taking nearly an hour for meditation. He set himself
heavy spiritual reading, going through St. John of the Cross's
Ascent of Mount Carmel and the first parts of the *Dark
Night*, which he was reading for the second time.

Tom liked getting up before dawn to pray according to the
Rule. Christian monks from earliest times had modeled a
Rule for their hours of prayer on the events of the last
twenty-four hours of Christ's life. The Passover dinner was
Mass. Then came the night prayers in the Garden of Geth-
semani, the pre-dawn prayers before the kiss of betrayal and

the arrest. Then came the prayers for the hours of that last day. They embraced the twenty-four hours of the monk's life, day and night. The "Little Hours" which Tom got up before dawn each day to pray began with Prime. Prime was the name of the "first hour," about 6 A.M. It included prayers of thanks for the light of approaching day, and asked blessings on the day's work ahead. Then came Terce, about 9 A.M., then Sext, about noon, and None at 3 P.M. These were the prayers known as the "Little Hours"—called "Little Hours" because they are short, about fifteen minutes. These four hours were spaced throughout the day, and followed by Vespers at 5:30 P.M., lasting half an hour. Then supper. Compline was the prayer said before retiring. Matins, or Vigils, was the night prayer—contemplative monks rose at 2 or 3 A.M. for Vigils. This entire ritual of prayer had one name: the Divine Office.

During those fall days, Tom more and more sought to resolve the spiritual need in his life. Could he give up everything? Could he be really poor? Not that he was so rich. As a professor of English at St. Bonaventure, he got forty-five dollars a month plus room and board. Yet he felt his life was rich.

"How can I write about poverty when, though I am in a way poor, yet I still live as though in a country club?"

He turned to the Bible. "I suddenly got a notion which shows that I was not very far advanced in the spiritual life. I thought of praying God to let me know what I was going to do, or what I should do . . . by showing it to me in the Scriptures." He opened the Bible, blindly put his finger on a page, and when he looked the words were:

"*Ecce eris tacens*, Behold, thou shalt be silent!"

He was thunderstruck. The first thought that came to him was that he was destined to be a Trappist. Then he told himself it was superstitious to make an oracle of the Bible. That was not to be done with Sacred Scripture.

In November the baroness returned. Tom went to meet her train with some of the priests, and when they were in the car, driving along the wet highway, the baroness said to him: "Well, Tom, when are you coming to Harlem for good?"

Taken aback, Tom began to say that his coming to Harlem depended on how much writing he could do there.

"Tom," said the baroness, "are you thinking of becoming a priest?"

"Oh, no, I have no vocation to the priesthood," he responded. Anyway—he added lamely—he couldn't do anything until February, as he had to finish the semester's teaching. Everyone laughed. But Tom was more perturbed than ever, and began to pray even harder. His soul ached with the question: "What shall I do? Where shall I go?"

At least he could go to Harlem and share his life with the suffering people, those despised as Christ had been despised. The baroness assured Tom he'd have plenty of time to write in the mornings while living at Friendship House. She expected him.

He had the sense of a deadline inside his soul, and that he was getting close to a decision. At the end of November he tried positive thinking. "The time has come for me to go and be a Trappist," he told himself with positive conviction. All he needed was somebody who could give him advice. But who?

In New York during Thanksgiving, he'd had lunch with Mark Van Doren at the Columbia Faculty Club. The main reason Tom wanted to see him was to talk about his novel. But it was not the novel that interested Mark Van Doren.

"What about your idea of being a priest?" he wanted to know. "Did you ever take that up again?"

Tom shrugged.

Mark said: "I talked about that to someone who knows what it is all about, and he said that the fact you let it all drop when you were told you had no vocation might really be a sign you had none."

It was like a smack in the face. Instead of putting the whole decision at God's door and fatalistically bowing to a supposed Will of God, Mark had put the decision right back on Tom. If you have a vocation, one sign might be that you don't give it up that easily! Tom was stung. What really hurt was that this came from Mark Van Doren who wasn't even a Catholic.

Merton said humbly: "I think God's Providence arranged things so that you would tell me that today."

Back at St. Bona's, Tom had a friend among the Franciscans, Father Philotheus, a gentle, cultured friar who had taught Tom the philosophy of St. Bonaventure. Tom went to the room that belonged to Father Philotheus, but when he got there, he suddenly ran away to the dark grove of trees along the west side of the football field.

In front of the shrine of the Little Flower, St. Thérèse of Lisieux, he knelt on the sharp gravel path. The trees dripped cold, wet tears on his head. He could not see the shrine in the darkness, but cried out to St. Thérèse: "For heaven's sake, help me!"

Then he got up and started back to the monastery. "I'll go in and ask Father Philotheus. I'll say, Here's the situation, Father, should I go and be a Trappist?"

But when he got to Father Philotheus's room, he still could not knock on the door. He was afraid that Father Philotheus might say: "Now look, you told the baroness that you would go and work with her at Friendship House in Harlem, and you can't go back on your word."

Tom knew that to go and work in Harlem was a good and reasonable way to follow Christ, and wouldn't that be exactly the way everybody would advise? But doing the good and reasonable thing wasn't for Tom; it was too much like the prudent giver. To do what was reasonable for Christ wouldn't be anything special—so, in that sense, going to live in Harlem didn't strike him as anything special.

He wanted to give more than what was reasonable, and becoming a Trappist was more. It was so exciting, he was filled with awe and painful desire.

He turned and ran all the way back to the grove, one idea hammering at his brain: "Give up everything, give up everything!"

In the woody grove, at the shrine of St. Thérèse, the dark was intense, and there was a silence, cold as the chilling rain.

"Please help me." He clasped his hands in anguish. "What am I going to do? I can't go on like this. Look at the state I am in. Show me the way. Show me what to do."

Suddenly in that strange silence a sound came, clear, not imaginary. It was a bell. The great bell in the big gray tower at Gethsemani was ringing.

The bell ringing in his ears, Tom turned and went, calmly now, back to see Father Philotheus.

"I want to be a Trappist."

"Are you sure you want to be a *Trappist?*" asked the priest.

"I want to give God everything."

Father Philotheus smiled and told Tom to go at once and send his request to the abbot of Gethsemani. Tom immediately wrote the abbot, asking permission to come for retreat at Christmas, hinting strongly that he was coming as a postulant. A few days later he heard from Gethsemani: Come.

At the end of the week, Tom was out walking, gazing at the hills and woods, the railway trestle over the river, the peaceful rural scene. As he turned back to the college, two other lay professors hurried to meet him and said: "Did you hear the radio?"

"No," said Tom.

"The Japanese bombed Pearl Harbor." It was Sunday, December 7, 1941. America was at war.

Tom was given permission to leave immediately for his Gethsemani retreat since his draft board might call him any time. He packed his clothes in a large box addressed to Baroness de Hueck at Friendship House; gave his books to Father Irenaeus and his library; tore up the manuscripts of his three and a half novels and threw them in the incinerator; sent his poems and a carbon copy of his "Journal of My Escape From the Nazis" (later published as *My Argument With the Gestapo*) to Mark Van Doren; put everything else he'd written in a binder addressed to Lax and Rice, who were sharing an apartment in New York; wrote three letters—one to Lax, one to the baroness, one to his family—and by evening, he was at the station.

The train from Buffalo came through freezing sleet, its whistle blowing plaintively in the dark of that winter's evening. Tom got on and sat down near the window. The train pulled out. The last city he could see out of the window was Erie, then he fell asleep exhausted, and slept right through Cleveland. But, in the middle of the night he woke up to say the rosary. For several months he'd been practicing getting up in the middle of the night in order to pray. Subconsciously he had been preparing to be a Trappist for months, practicing the prayer disciplines of those contemplative orders whose prayers go out when all others are asleep.

Riding this lonesome train in the middle of the night, Thomas Merton thought of Aldous Huxley, who had written the words that had brought him so early the first glimpse of mystical truth and the concept of selflessness and detachment required of those who seek it.

Aldous Huxley had sent money to Friendship House after reading about it in a review that Thomas Merton had written of one of Huxley's books. So they affected each other. Huxley mentioned Merton to his friend Christopher Isherwood, in a letter dated February 7, 1942, just a few months later: "If you are ever in New York, it might be worth your while to get in touch with a man, with whom I have exchanged one or two letters of late—a Catholic called Thomas Merton, whose address is St. Bonaventure, New York . . . He wrote very interestingly from a Catholic viewpoint about *Grey Eminence*, and described what sounds like a remarkable venture in saintliness functioning in Harlem among the poorest negroes. It is called Friendship House, 34 W. 135th Street, and is run by a woman called Catherine de Hueck, a Russian Catholic." There was a resonance between these two twentieth-century mystics. Both were men of rich literary and cultural background—Merton, the younger, sought in Catholicism what Huxley sought in Buddhism: a springboard for a high dive into the Infinite Sea. The shape of Western spirituality would be changed by them more than anyone can assess— Christian and Buddhist spirituality coming together in a way no one had thought possible.

Carrying a small suitcase, Thomas Merton entered the secret garden of the Trappist monastery. It was December 10, 1941; he was twenty-six years old. Tom knocked on the door.

The flowers of last spring were matted in the frozen gray grass, and an icy wind blew through him. There were no birds in last year's nests. The garden was a desert.

At St. Bonaventure, reading St. John of the Cross, Thérèse of Lisieux, and the Bible, which he loved most, brought him one clear signal: a person seeking the spiritual encounter must prepare to cross a desert.

Saints and mystics had various names for this desert, which they explain as the emptying of Self. Teresa of Avila called it Nada. To St. John of the Cross is was Darkness, to Thérèse of Lisieux the desert was Littleness, and to Thomas Merton it was Nowhereness.

"For each of us there is a point of nowhereness in the middle of movement, a point of nothingness in the midst of being: the incomparable point. . . . If you seek it you do not find it. If you stop seeking it is there. But you must not turn to it. Once you become aware of yourself as seeker, you are lost. But if you are content to be lost you will be found without knowing it."

Words from the Bible came to him, Hebrews 11:40. He had even memorized chapter and verse. They were words written about the faith and the suffering of former saints who got lost in the desert: "All these having borne witness to the faith, did not receive what was promised, because God foresaw something better for us, that apart from us they should not be made perfect."

Pondering the passage of scripture, Tom knew he, too, was part of the promise: "And in turn I will suffer and prepare the way for others." He felt spiritually elated to think that such was the movement of the Bible. The Book of God was not completed because it was waiting for him, and all the others, who had to be "made perfect."

He realized there were those who didn't think he was evolving spiritually by becoming a monk. His literary agent expressed what many felt.

"I imagined this author of so much promise was now lost forever behind a high stone wall of silence. It seemed particularly sad because he had so passionately wanted to be published and had never doubted for one minute that he was destined to be a successful author."

The *I Ching* describes the twofold possibility granted the type of person who has been charged with the grandeur of God. This kind of person can rise to the heights of fame, can play an important part in the world. Or, such a person can withdraw into solitude and develop himself. He can go the way of the hero or of the sage. There is no general law to say which of the two is the right way.

The door opened. A monk stood looking at Tom. It was the guest master, Father Joachim. "Oh, it's you," he said.

"Yes, Father, I want to be a novice."

9

Sweet brother, if I do not sleep
My eyes are flowers for your tomb . . .

Tom felt the cold and the tomblike silence, as Father Joachim closed the door behind him. The building was icy and the place seemed empty. He was inside. But he was not yet inside the monastery where the monks lived, for he was not even a postulant (a candidate for admission). He was a guest, and Father Joachim, the guest master, showed him to a private room like any other guest, or nearly. Tom looked around the room assigned to him. He looked down at himself, at the blue suit he was wearing. Soon, perhaps in a few days, he would take off these clothes, never to wear them again.

A young man who comes to Gethsemani to be a monk must first be accepted as a postulant. After a couple of months he would become a novice, learning the rudiments of Trappist life for a period of two years. Then he could make temporary "simple vows" for three more years. Altogether, he would be on probation for five years, if he lasted that long.

He put his suitcase down and hastened to the church. Inside the huge nave, the cold was like that in an arctic cave.

Tom knelt and prayed. After that, it was time for supper—scrambled eggs and cheese and milk. It was a guesthouse meal, not the typical monks' fare which would be more like potato soup and barley coffee.

An old man sat across from him at the table, hunched up in a sweater. He, too, was a would-be postulant. The next day he was gone. But another candidate for admission, a fat youth—Tom called him "Fat Boy"—stayed until Lent.

Tom was set to work, with the other candidate for admission, to wax floors and wash dishes—in silence. For the silence, Tom was grateful; he didn't wish to talk.

That night before lying down to sleep Tom looked into the Spiritual Directory Father Joachim had left in his room.

A Trappist monastery consists of a community of men leading a silent life of prayer and penance, liturgy and study, manual labor and fasting—consecrated to God. The life is hard. The night is broken hours of sleep interspersed with risings for prayer. One has to drag oneself out of a deep sleep in the darkest hours before dawn to go and pray. The beds of straw and boards are a help—they make it easier to get up.

The monastery at Gethsemani, in the knob country of Kentucky, was built around the time of the Civil War. It is a few miles from Abraham Lincoln's birthplace.

In the history of Gethsemani, it is written that Father Paulinus struck a bargain for fourteen hundred acres of woodland with some log cabins in bad repair. The land was sold to the Trappists for five thousand dollars, and in October of 1848, a band of French monks from Melleray arrived to carry the Holy Name and the holy worship of God into the forests of North America, "among the tigers and panthers and wolves of Kentucky." That most of the tigers and panthers and wolves of Kentucky were spiritual did not make them any less fearful.

"When a man becomes a Cistercian," Thomas Merton wrote in the original manuscript of The Seven Storey Mountain, "he is stripped not only of his clothes, or part of his skin, but of his whole body and most of his spirit as well. And it is not finished the first day: far from it! The whole Cistercian life is an evisceration, a gutting and scouring of the human soul. The exchange of secular clothes for a religious habit is symbolic . . . the symbol represents the interior stripping."

Within a few days after Tom had arrived at the monastery, the master of novices, called Father Master, came upstairs and told Tom and Fat Boy to get their things together. They got their bags and followed Father Master downstairs and into the room occupied by Dom Frederic, the abbot, the man who had absolute authority over the monastery and everybody in it. He was deep in the pile of letters and papers which covered his desk like a mountain of work. They knelt by his desk. Then Dom Frederic turned to them and told them they would make the community either better or worse. It all depended on them. He blessed them and they kissed his ring and went out, as he called after them to be joyful but not dissipated.

At the other end of the long hall they went into a room where they handed over their suitcases, fountain pens, wristwatches, and any cash on hand. Then they signed documents promising that if they left the monastery they would not sue the monks for wages for their manual labor. Only then were they permitted to cross the threshold of the monks' private world and enter the long wing in the back of the building where the monks lived. Immediately they felt everything was warmer. The atmosphere was full of vibrancy, there was a smell of warm bread coming from the bakery, the monks moved about with their cowls over their arms, at ease. The two postulants entered the tailor shop to be measured for their robes.

A few days later Tom was called in by Father Master and given an armful of white woolen garments. He had to master the complications of the fifteenth-century underwear Trappists wore under their robes, but soon he emerged from the room wearing a white robe, a white cloth band tied around his waist, and a white shapeless cloak around his shoulders.

As a parallel to the stripping of his worldly clothes, he now began the interior stripping. He was not a guest, but one of the community of men hidden in white cowls and brown capes. Some monks had beards, others had monastic crowns (shaven heads). There were young men and old men; all were silent. They were not without laughter, but silence was the rule and they were obedient, because obedience was also the rule.

At fourteen, Tom had refused to run with the pack. That summer in Scotland he had refused to submit his will to those in authority. Now Tom accepted the vow of obedience as a particularly perfect instrument for self-stripping. Indeed, he saw it as even more perfect when the obedience required was not reasonable.

"Every trial, even the smallest, every opportunity to deny ourselves, every chance to offer some kind of sacrifice, is to be regarded as a grace, as a favor, as a providential opportunity to grasp at freedom."

From the first instant, the graces of misery poured down on Tom like a hard rain. Saints are said to despise "consolations," but Tom refused to despise these buoyant levitations of his soul. He didn't care if consolations were considered a weakness that strong souls can do without. He accepted the joys with the miseries.

"Love sails me around the house. I walk two steps on the ground and four steps in the air. It is love. It is consolation. I don't care if it is consolation. I am not attached to consolation. I love God. Love carries me around. I don't want to *do* anything but love. And when the bell rings it is like pulling teeth to make myself shift because of that love, secret love, hidden love, obscure love, down inside me and outside me where I don't care to talk about it."

There were bells always ringing, monastery bells, bells calling him to get out of bed, bells calling him to prayer, bells calling him to work, bells calling him to eat; bells bells bells.

Love made obedience all right, even when Tom didn't agree with rules. From the first he didn't agree with the rigidity of the Trappist order, and he went right on disagreeing while being perfect in obedience. His refusal to make excuses for what was childish in religious regulations, while at the same time submitting spiritually for the sake of the discipline, made him powerful. It gave him the spiritual energy to work for the long overdue reforms which the coming of Pope John XXIII made explicit for all religious orders.

"Those were hard years. . . . It was a period of training, and a happy, austere one. . . . The best Gethsemani poems belong to this period."

Having been warned that the austerities practiced by the Trappists were beyond human endurance, Tom set about toughening himself that first week at Gethsemani. One day the master of novices came to see him in his room. There sat Tom, reading the Spiritual Directory with the window wide open.

"Aren't you cold in here? Why don't you shut the window?"

"Warm as toast," stuttered the brave young postulant.

"Well, close the window anyway."

As a postulant he received a new name to signify the new man come to birth in Thomas Merton. The name was Louis. He didn't know who Louis was, but anyway he was glad he didn't get Sylvester. The other postulant got Sylvester.

When a man entered the monastery, he was summoned before the community of monks and asked the ritual question "*Quid petis?* What do you seek?"

The seeker who answered "happiness" was out. If he answered "contemplation," that was even worse—that was as bad as answering "desire to escape from society."

"If I had a secret desire for what the lingo of the pious manuals would call the 'summits' I had better be cautious about the way I manifested it," Tom realized immediately. Prayer was the life he had come for, but he had better watch it.

Wit and humor were more typical of the monks than pietistic ways. They all kidded each other in sign languages that made the novices explode sometimes in sudden laughter. Later, when Thomas Merton was asked by his abbot to write Cistercian history, he discovered the same humor in the early accounts of monastic life.

In the beginning of the American foundation, when the monastery was still under the old French system, cleanliness was not next to godliness. Holy men weren't considered holy if they were too hygiene-minded. And even in the first half of the twentieth century, young applicants discovered there were only two showers in the monastery.

Laundry facilities, too, were not then up to date. The monks' habits went unwashed for long periods of time. Wit marks the accounts of the winter habits and how they got holier and holier as layer of sweat was added to moldy layer of sweat. Like soldiers on a battlefield, the monks reacted with humor to these hardships.

In all the time he was at Gethsemani, Thomas Merton said he never had any temptation to leave the monastery. Others gave up; Tom stayed. He had one thing going for him in particular—he did not fear loneliness.

"Are our efforts to be more 'communal' and to be more 'family,' really genuine, or are they only new ways to be intolerant of the solitude and integrity of the individual person . . . trying to submerge and absorb him, and keep him from finding an identity that might express itself in dissent?"

One temptation alone haunted him when it came to a question of leaving Gethsemani: the temptation to be a hermit.

The first Christmas Tom experienced at Gethsemani, the monks got up, not at two in the morning as was their usual way but at nine in the evening, having gone to bed earlier, at five.

The winter night was not far along and the paralyzing cold of the small hours not yet pervasive. The monks went into the church where the crib was lit with a soft glow. A forest of cedar branches surrounded the altar. Matins, or the night office, began. As the solemn Gregorian phrases mounted, their cadences rocked the church, as though the angels had joined in the singing: "Gloria in Excelsis" showering upon the earth from the stars messages of peace. The church glowed with fierce intensity.

"Suddenly I was in a new world. I seemed to be the same person, and I was the same person, I was still myself, I was more myself than I had ever been, and yet I was nothing. It was as if the floor had fallen out of my soul and I was free to go in and out of infinity. . . . I could rest in this dark unfathomable peace . . . the mind was not all excluded . . .

the mind too could enter into the peace and harmony of this infinite simplicity that had come to be born within me."

The nights of prayer and spiritual élan went with days of work. The monks were building a dam. Their axes echoed over the water, and while working Tom would glance up through the trees at the spire of the abbey church with the long blue ridge of hills behind it.

On the first Sunday of Lent, Tom stood before Father Abbot with the other postulant who had entered at the same time. Father Abbot was ill with pneumonia, but this did not keep him from delivering an impassioned lecture in a hoarse voice which made his words all the more moving. He warned them that if they came to Gethsemani seeking anything but the cross they were making a mistake, for sickness, humiliations, fasts, and sufferings were what Gethsemani offered.

Two weeks later, Tom went to the infirmary with influenza.

"Now at last I will have some solitude and plenty of time to pray," he thought happily.

In bed, he opened the Bible and began reading with the voracious pleasure of the addicted reader who has long been denied. Monasteries, Tom was discovering, resisted the pure contemplative. There was an exaggerated reverence for baking bread, for making cheese, for chopping wood, for planting crops. Communal prayer was richly central to the life, and the Divine Office made necessary that monks pray throughout the day and night. But little consideration was given to doing nothing—pure contemplation tended to be distrusted as "idleness."

One of the first things Father Master had done when Tom entered the monastery was dispel Tom's idea that he was to give up writing. He ordered Tom to write! The time between four and five-thirty in the morning, in the great silence after the night office, was wonderful for writing poetry. After two or three hours of prayer, he found his mind was saturated in the peace and richness of the liturgy. As dawn came, whole blocks of imagery crystallized out of the darkness and silence. Then Father Master found out. He told Tom that he should write, but he should also keep the Rule. The Rule required that those dawn hours be sacred for the study of scripture and the psalms, not for writing poetry.

Thomas Merton had the happy gift of turning every happening in his monastic life, even serious deprivations, into greater fulfillments. Thus he found that Father Master had actually endowed him with an opportunity for a creativity even more exhilarating than writing poems before dawn: the opportunity for meditation!

"What a time that is for reading and meditation! . . . in the summer when you can take your book and go out under the trees. What shades of light and color fill the woods . . . and in the east the dawn sky is a blaze of fire where you might almost expect to see the winged animals of Ezekiel."

For many years he always meditated at that time of day and read St. Augustine, St. Gregory, St. Ambrose on the psalms and the Bible. "As soon as I had entered into the world of these great saints . . . I lost all desire to prefer that time for any writing of my own."

The harmony of a life whose days were integrated with both natural and supernatural cycles was rewarding. That first summer, Tom learned the art of pitching hay.

To lift up a shock of hay on the fork and to pitch the shock just where it belonged on the big wagon wasn't easy. After the big wagons were loaded, two or three novices would ride back and help unload the shocks. That was the hardest job of all.

"In about two minutes the place begins to put on a very good imitation of purgatory, for the sun is beating down mercilessly on a tin roof over your head, and the loft is one big black stifling oven. I wish I had thought a little about that cow barn, back in the days when I was committing so many sins."

The woods sizzled under Kentucky's fierce summer sun. A thousand crickets sent out their high shrill. In choir, the flies buzzed, bit, crawled over lips and forehead and into sweat-stung eyes. Novices, seeing penance with new understanding, departed. Tom stayed on.

"I don't think I enjoyed the heat any more than anybody else, but with my active temperament, I could satisfy myself that all my work and all my sweat really meant something, because they made me feel as if I were doing something for God."

Coming home from haying he looked at the blue evening over the valley surrounding the monastery and said: "Anybody who runs away from a place like this is crazy."

While Thomas Merton was still teaching at St. Bonaventure, his brother had crossed the border into Canada and joined the Royal Canadian Air Force. Knowing that John Paul would fly a bomber as dangerously as he drove a car, Tom had immediately put John Paul in the care of St. Thérèse of Lisieux. Now John Paul wrote that he was coming in the fall to see Tom at Gethsemani. He had got his sergeant stripes and was being sent overseas—he would come to Gethsemani before he sailed.

As the days went by, Tom awaited his brother's arrival, worrying each day that John Paul would come while Tom was in some faraway cornfield and nobody would know where to find him. But as it happened, that particular afternoon he was assigned to weed a turnip patch right next to the monastery. A monk came out and signaled him. Tom knew his brother had at last arrived.

For the next few days the brothers talked and talked, and as they talked, the years dissolved. Tom recalled how serene a baby John Paul had been, how he would lie upstairs in the house his parents had rented in Flushing, Long Island. The baby would lie in his crib upstairs singing. It came back to Tom vividly, that sound—his brother humming a little singsong in his crib. Downstairs, his mother and father and he would listen, smiling, as the baby sang and the sun slanted through the windows.

After the loss of their mother, life had gotten more and more complicated for the boys—back and forth to Europe, over to England, to France, always on the move, rushing headlong from one complication to another. Tom remembered the bragging letters about all his dating, necking, spending, drinking. He had long felt responsible because he set the pattern of behavior for John Paul's wildness. The younger brother strove to outdo Tom, modeling himself after his elder, so that his college life at Cornell was as disastrous as

Tom's at Cambridge. Now both of them were making it up to each other, for John Paul wanted to be a Catholic, too, and had come with that in mind.

"Was there any possibility of happiness without some principle that transcended everything we had ever known? The house in Douglaston, which my grandparents had built, and which they maintained for twenty-five years with the ice-box constantly full . . . fifteen different kinds of magazines on the living room table and a Buick in the garage. . . ."

These, the signs of middle-class American affluence and status, hadn't brought happiness—just the opposite. The two brothers had been constantly running from the house and each other, to movies, bars, driving at top speed, flying planes, going places. They had everything except inner sub-stance—they were the hollow men that T. S. Eliot wrote about. The "gift of faith" which filled the hollowness for Tom was a gift he could at last share with John Paul. So, prepared with a cram course of instruction, John Paul was baptized into the Catholic Church.

On the morning of the baptism, Tom walked to the chapel of Our Lady of Victories. The church seemed empty as he entered and looked for his brother. Then he saw John Paul in the Royal Canadian Air Force uniform, kneeling, far down the nave. There, in the empty church, with just the two of them, Tom seemed to see once more—as he looked down the long nave—the small boy standing in a field, who wanted to come over to the board-and-tarpaper house Tom and his pals had built for their clubhouse. Tom had chased him away, but the five-year-old, in his short pants and leather jacket, wouldn't go. He just stood, his arms hanging down at his sides, afraid to come nearer because of the stones they threw. Tom shouted beat it, go home, and shied another rock in his direction, but John Paul wouldn't. He stood there, not cry-ing, just indignant and angry, his eyes looking into Tom's with great hurt.

The next morning, after the baptism in the chapel of Our Lady of Victories, John Paul was off. A visitor at the abbey was giving him a ride to Bardstown. The brothers said good-by. Tom stood at the gate and watched the car go down the avenue. His brother turned around once and waved.

Christmas came, then New Year's, and then Thomas Merton's twenty-eighth birthday. After that, Lent arrived quickly. Tom was determined that this Lent he'd make the fast without breaking down as he had the year before.

The monks ate nothing until noon, then had two bowls, one of soup and the other of vegetables, and as much bread as they liked. In the evening they had "a light collation"—bread and two ounces of applesauce. This was Lenten fare.

Tom soon discovered that swinging a sledge hammer on an empty stomach could make your knees shaky. Dom Frederic then decided Tom could do more for the order as a writer than as a swinger of sledge hammers. He set him to work translating books and articles from the French. And so day followed day and the liturgy of penance arrived at Holy Week. The monks went about the cloisters barefooted. On Holy Thursday came the ritual washing of the feet in imitation of Christ washing the feet of Peter. The monks washed the feet of poor men who came into the cloister, then kissed their hands and feet and gave them dinner. On Good Friday, the sad Lamentations were cried, the words of Christ on the cross: "Oh my people how have I offended you?" After that came Holy Saturday's great bells, ringing in the Resurrection, and the responding voices of the monks singing out their alleluias.

Easter was late that year, the twenty-fifth of April. On Holy Saturday Tom saw a letter from John Paul and two or three other letters under the napkin in the refectory, but monks may neither send nor receive letters during Lent so he did not open his mail until the Monday following Easter Sunday.

Then he learned that John Paul had married, having fallen in love with an English girl. He had his wife went to the Lakes for a week, the letter said, and he was presently at a new base and had already been on bombing missions twice.

Next day, Tom was writing his answer to John Paul. The Father Master entered and signed Tom to go to the abbot. When Tom entered, the abbot read him a telegram. John Paul had been reported missing in action on April seventeenth.

Tom never found out why it took ten days for that telegram to reach him. It was weeks before he learned the details. Then he found out that on a Friday night, the sixteenth of April, John Paul and his crew had taken off for Mannheim. The plane went down in the North Sea. John Paul, terribly injured, nevertheless supported the pilot, keeping both of them afloat (he didn't know the pilot was already dead). When his companions pulled him into the rubber dinghy, he lay in the bottom, delirious, asking for water. The water tank had broken in the crash and there was none. After three hours of great suffering, John Paul died. He was buried at sea. Five days later the survivors were rescued.

"Sweet brother, if I do not sleep, my eyes are flowers for your tomb" is the first sentence of the poem Thomas Merton wrote on the death of his brother.

It was only after John Paul's death that the great power of Merton as a writer of personal existence was fulfilled. He came to have readers in every part of the world, and would one day be regarded as one of the most remarkable spiritual forces to be generated in the United States, just through the intense personalism of his writings.

Eighteen years after the death of John Paul, a young postulant from Canada was set to work with a wrecking bar, smashing up the partitions of the room in the old guesthouse on the third floor. "He is the son of an airman who married an English girl, as my brother did, during the war," wrote Thomas Merton. "He was born in the Blitz, in England. And now he is tearing down that room and my own history—a fact which I gladly accept, but with this sense of loss nevertheless! Eighteen years since the three survivors in John Paul's crew dropped his body off the lifeboat into the North Sea. His back was broken when the plane hit the surface."

The Christmas after John Paul's death, Tom was assisting in the celebration of the Mass. He looked out and saw Bob Lax. He was taking communion! He had become a Catholic.

When Lax returned to New York, he took the manuscript of Thomas Merton's poems with him. This was a turning point in Tom's literary and spiritual life.

James Laughlin of New Directions publishing house accepted the poems. The published volume, *Thirty Poems*, appeared at the end of November 1944.

Tom took the printed copy of his book and walked out under the November sky to the edge of the cemetery. He stood in the icy wind. It was a snow sky, dark and threatening.

He was happy and sad. Having found his identity as a monk, would he lose it now by becoming known as a writer? He had not yet come to the completion of his simple vows. When he entered the Cistercian monastery, he had been first a postulant, then a novice for two years. Then he had taken simple vows for three years. After that, when he had finished five years of spiritual schooling, he'd either make his solemn perpetual vows or leave. If he stayed the five years, he would be ordained a priest.

Tom knew he would never want to return to the everyday world. He wished to go out farther, to become a hermit. Was writing consistent with the deepening of spiritual experience? If not he would give up writing. No, said his abbot, Dom Frederic, Tom was to write. He wanted him to write a great many books.

But Tom wanted to write not just out of obedience to his abbot, or for the enlightenment of the religious. He wanted to write what he himself wanted to write. He realized that this was selfish, so he went to confession and confessed that he had this terrible, selfish temptation—the temptation to write his autobiography.

10

The rabbits stayed quiet until we threw holy water at them and then they all jumped.

Now everything changed for Tom. The autobiography that he had gone to his confessor about had come up against resistance. His confessor had laughed at such an idea. One of the censors of the order was even more critical and suggested Tom take a course in grammar first. With his acceptance of the vow of obedience, Tom felt he had to submit. The vow of obedience required submission to superiors, whether the superiors were right or wrong. You submitted yourself to their prejudices as well as to their ideals. Getting rejected was part of the stripping away of the interior man.

Luckily, Dom Frederic insisted that Tom write—poems, history, articles, and also his autobiography. In fact, the abbot wouldn't let Tom stop writing, so that by the time Tom made his solemn vows—the year preceding his ordination—he had written himself into a state of collapse. He'd finished the life of a great Trappistine woman, Mother Berchmans, while at the same time writing *The Ascent to Truth, The Seeds of Contemplation, The Waters of Siloe*, numberless poems, short articles, research essays, a new postulant's guide, a revised history of the Cistercian order, and his autobiography, *The Seven Storey Mountain*.

No wonder he became hysterical on the morning he made his solemn vows. He lay on the floor in the middle of the church, face down, and while Father Abbot was praying over him Tom began to laugh. The humor had hit him. Here he was, the silent Trappist, the wordless contemplative, pouring out a hundred words a minute!

The paradox was that writing tied in with contemplation. He decided that the important thing was not to live for contemplation, but to live for God, and the rest was amazing grace.

On May 23, 1949, Thomas Merton wrote in his journal: "In three days, if I am alive, and if the Archbishop does not fall down and break his leg, I should be a priest." He could hardly realize it: "I shall say Mass—I shall say Mass."

Three days later, the Archbishop not having fallen down and broken a leg, Thomas Merton—aged thirty-four—was ordained a priest. After he said his first Mass he was so exalted, he cried: "The Mass is the most wonderful thing that has ever entered my life. When I am at the altar I feel that I am at last the person God has truly intended me to be." He never got over his exaltation, and he made sure of saying Mass each day. He'd also made out his will, giving up everything.

"Yesterday morning I made my will. You always make a will before solemn vows, getting rid of everything, as if you were about to die," he noted in his journal.

Then no sooner had he renounced earthly things than Father Abbot called him in and gave him a telegram: "Manuscript accepted. Happy New Year." The telegram was signed by the editor-in-chief of Harcourt Brace, who turned out to be Tom's old Columbia schoolmate, Bob Giroux. Not much later, Father Abbot presented Tom with the contract.

"So after making my will I put my living signature on this contract. The royalties of the dead author will go to the monastery. Meanwhile I spent the afternoon writing business letters and making all kinds of mistakes."

Three days before Tom's final vows, the wardrobe keeper went up to the attic and came down with the suitcase Tom had brought with him to the monastery. Tom had to check over the clothes and see that everything was there. Then he formally renounced all his worldly gear—a blue woolen sweater, four striped sports shirts, the blue suit he had been wearing when he entered the monastery, and the suitcase that still had a shiny blue-and-white Cuba Mail Line label on it.

But of course lots of things had been changing in the years since he had arrived at the monastery. Gethsemani was changing.

A few months before Tom was ready to be ordained, a revolution had been introduced into the monastery—self-shaving. For the first time in a century, the monks of Gethsemani were given brushes and safety razors and small bars of soap and even (despite the danger to their vanity) mirrors. That was the end of the communal electric shave. No longer would the monks have to sit around waiting their turn. They were allowed to shave twice a week, and began hacking away at their own chins.

Another revolution, at least in Tom's life, was that he was given the use of the rare-book vault for his writing. A private study at last! The place had two steel doors and was nearly soundproof. Considering how noisy the Trappist monastery had become with all the building developments, the rare-book vault was incredibly attractive.

"How quiet it is in the vault. I open a top window and you see nothing but a little square of blue Kentucky sky and the sun streams in on the bindings of the codices and the big quartos . . . everything is silent and you are steeped in the presence of God until it makes you numb."

There were also new problems. "America has discovered the contemplative life," said Merton. Undoubtedly the dropping of the atom bomb on Hiroshima on August 6, 1945, played a profound part.

The abbey had been planned for about seventy men. Now 270 seekers were packed into the building. Literally, there were wall-to-wall monks. Does such a big crowd really make for "community"? Tom wondered.

New buildings had to go up. Expansion could be achieved faster by using machines, so very soon the monks were no longer doing the building they had once done with their own hands. A small mechanized army of builders took over. Mechanical monsters pursued silent walkers in the woods. A D-4 Traxcavator, enormous, biting into the earth with huge gulps, devouring everything in sight and roaring all the time, was described by Tom as having "a face like a drawbridge." Daughter houses were being founded in Georgia, in Utah, and in New Mexico as a partial solution to the overcrowding.

In the eye of the hurricane, Thomas Merton went on writing, peacefully creating an American spirituality that reflected the indigenous American theme of the lonely search by the lonely seeker in the midst of the lonely crowd of extroverts accumulating things.

Out of Tom's monastic life he was creating a literature of spirituality that had been heretofore solely the mode of the American poets and novelists. He was making articulate the religious soul of a people long described as spiritually shallow when compared with European and Asian mystics.

Tom felt that the years at Gethsemani were going too fast. The Cistercian life was energetic, and sometimes he felt that it was too energetic. The monastery had grown and the cheese-making had become more and more important. People from the outside world were ordering cheese from Gethsemani, as if the cheese in itself would make them holy. This made Tom remark sarcastically: "We seem to think that God will not be satisfied with a monastery that does not behave in every way like a munitions factory under wartime conditions of production." One young monk put a notice on the monastery bulletin board: "All my cheeses for Jesus."

Laughter made for balance, and there was plenty of laughter. Sometimes Tom could not restrain his own tendency to be a comedian. "I should not have made funny faces when Fr. Appolinaris said Abraham was born 1,959 years after the creation of the world," he told himself sternly.

His sense of humor burst out in the holiest places. When the monks were chanting the evening prayer for the Vespers of the Virgin Mary's birthday and sang: "*Coeli fenestra facta es,* Thou art become the window of heaven," the fountain of laughter bubbled up and Tom said: "I am glad that in our

Order we still enter heaven through the window. I believe that the line of the hymn was reformed in the Roman liturgy so that the rest of the Church goes in more decorously through the door. But we Cistercians still get in by the window." The idea appealed to Tom, perhaps because it seemed less respectable than going into heaven by a door! Sometimes he could not even be respectful of solemn functions, especially where the music played reminded him of the music heard in the days of silent movies. "Weird music on the organ," he would comment.

Tom was happy to discover he was not the only Trappist who suffered from shoddy religious music and shoddy religious art. Dom Gabriel Sortais, the Vicar General, came from France, and he confided to Tom that in the rooms where he had to stay he used to take all the religious statues and pictures and hide them in a closet. They made him sick.

Merton felt exactly that way about literature. "A bad book about the love of God remains a bad book, even though it may be about the love of God."

That year even the valleys and fields were filled with exaltation. Tom noted in his journal that he and Father Macarius went out and blessed the fields on Ascension Day in May 1948. When they got to the cow pasture, the calves really looked impressed as he and Father Macarius blessed them, and even the pigs took an active interest. But not the sheep, who showed no spirit of concern, and the chickens ran away as if aggrieved. But the rabbits were the most responsive —"the rabbits stayed quiet," that is, "until we threw holy water at them, and then they all jumped."

On July 7, 1948, *The Seven Storey Mountain* was published. Reverend Father, with a look of profound satisfaction, handed Tom the first copy. Tom went off alone and began to skim through it. He began to feel queasy. "Where did I get all that pious rhetoric?" he wondered.

He never got over the shock of reading, in print, the style of writing which critics were to admire and call "prophetic." He was not content with the idea that his style was "prophetic"; he should not use religion as a way of passing judgment. Twenty years later, writing a new preface for the Japanese edition of *The Seven Storey Mountain*, he commented that since the time when he had first written the book he had learned "to look upon the world with more compassion."

Chosen as the selection of three book clubs, *The Seven Storey Mountain* immediately went into a second printing. Tom laughed and wondered if it would be bought by the movies.

Some friends of Merton's became indignant about the church getting all of Tom's money. When he entered the monastery he had taken a vow of poverty, but why should the monastery get money that was Tom's? Here, too, Tom reacted in his own unique way. He was thankful the monastery had the worry of the money. That left him with only one worry—the pleasure he took in being a famous author. Who cared for the money! The big thing was that he'd written a book that was being read by millions of people.

"I suppose, since I was the author of the book, I must take responsibility for *The Seven Storey Mountain*. But there was one man who was in a certain sense even more responsible for that book than I was, even as he was the cause of all my other writing. That man was Dom Frederic Dunne, my spiritual Father, the abbot who had received me as a postulant, who had given me the habit of novice one cold Sunday in Lent when he himself was nearly dying of pneumonia, who had received me to simple and to solemn profession. It was Dom Frederic who had formed and shaped my whole monastic destiny. . . ."

Dom Frederic's work was done. He had seen *The Seven Storey Mountain*—the book which meant more to him than to its author—at last appear in print. Almost as soon as the book came out, he died.

It happened in August. He went to Georgia on the night train and had not yet returned when Tom came down to choir. Tom was anxious, and prayed that his abbot was all right. Later, the prior told the monks that Dom Frederic was dead. He had died on the night train to Georgia.

Just the day before, Tom had seen him alive, spoken with him, and Dom Frederic had expressed his joy over Tom's writing. He had taken much time to reassure Tom about his literary success, and to tell him there was no contradiction in his being both a monk and a writer. He told Tom that the contemplative life was in his writing. He would communicate the spirit of prayer to many people and help many to penetrate the mystery of the love of God.

The Vicar General of the order, Dom Gabriel Sortais, arrived just in time for Dom Frederic Dunne's funeral and to preside over the election of a new abbot.

Dom Gabriel Sortais could not speak English. As Merton's second language was French, he was assigned the job of interpreting for him. The Vicar General had to go into Louisville one day and he asked to have Tom go along as his interpreter. Thus it was that, for the first time in seven years, Thomas Merton emerged from behind the gates of the monastery.

He felt strange. It had been a long time since he had left the world, and it seemed longer. He wondered if the world of human commerce was still as revolting as when he had entered the monastery. Perhaps the old sarcasm would be all he could muster.

But Gethsemani had changed Thomas Merton. As they came into Louisville, the world of humanity which he had once seen as corrupt and driven by shallow ambitions, did not appear that way any more. The people looked sad, worn-out; even when happy they had a pathos in their expressions. He realized he could no longer see people as he once had.

"In Louisville, at the corner of Fourth and Walnut, in the center of the shopping district, I was suddenly overwhelmed with the realization that I loved all those people, that they were mine and I theirs, that we could not be alien to one another even though we were total strangers. It was like waking from a dream of separateness, of spurious self-isolation in a special world, the world of renunciation and supposed holiness."

The only way monks were different was that they took a different attitude toward the things of the world—to bombs, to race hatred, to big business. But they were in the same world as everybody else; just the attitude was different. Realizing this, Tom felt such a sharp sense of liberation that he laughed out loud, standing there on the corner of Fourth and Walnut, and cried, "Thank God, thank God, that I *am* like other men, that I am only a man among others."

Instead of resigning from the human race in order to be a monk, he had become a monk in order to enter it, ". . . a race dedicated to many absurdities and one which makes many terrible mistakes; yet, with all that, God Himself gloried in becoming a member of the human race."

Merton's fan mail poured into the monastery, swelling to huge proportions. Dom Frederic had always helped Tom with his mail, but the new abbot, Dom James, gave Tom the task of answering all his own mail. Tom felt deeply responsible because the letters were good; they were serious and sensitive and not at all ridiculous.

On the first anniversary of Dom Frederic's death, Merton sat down near his grave under the trees filled with August locusts. He thought about his priesthood. It was only "the beginning of a journey, not its end," and he looked back over the rugged path he had taken.

He saw his life at Gethsemani as falling into different periods. The first was when he was a novice, 1942–1944. These were the years when radiators were not in favor in the monastery. The smell of the frozen straw during those winters in the icy dormitory was unforgettable. The second period was from his first vows to his ordination in 1949, "the one great secret for which I had been born." He had reached the moment of his highest intensity. Then, in the winter and Lent of 1949, he suddenly discovered that he was scarcely able to write at all. The strenuous labors, long hours of research, writing so many books and essays, and attending conferences, had drained him to the breaking point. He could not sleep. Night after night he lay awake on his bed of straw.

"You lie down in your dormitory cell and listen to first one monk and then another monk begin to snore, without, however, going to sleep yourself. Then you count the quarter hours by the tower clock and console yourself with an exact knowledge of the amount of sleep you are missing. The fun does not really begin until you get up at 2 A.M. and try to keep awake in choir."

He tried to use insomnia-time for contemplation, but could only lie there suffering, helpless, alone, and let himself be crushed by the tyranny of time.

"The plank bed becomes an altar and you lie there without trying to understand any longer in what sense you can be called a sacrifice."

Tiresome questions plucked at his mind: "Is it an act of virtue for a contemplative to sit down and let himself be snowed under by activities?" "Just because a cross is a cross does it follow that it is the cross God intends for you?"

He thought that he would never write again. For a year and a half, he could not even lift a pen. But after sufficient time had passed, he got well. His strength returned. As if there was no mercy for such a sinner, he was given more jobs than ever.

In 1951, he was made Master of the Scholastics. He had to teach young monks studying to be priests. Next, he was made Master of the Choir Novices and was even further involved in lectures and discussions and conferences for monks and priests. His teaching led him deeper into scriptural studies, as he had to prepare for his students, and in these studies he found a refreshment and exaltation that fed his spirit.

"I have a great reverence and love for the Patriarchs of the Old Testament—Abraham, Isaac, Jacob—and for the prophets —Samuel, Elias, Eliseus. When I walk in the cemetery in the cool evening when the sun is going down—there is almost no sunlight left now in the interval after supper—I think of Isaac, meditating in the fields at the evening and of Rebecca coming to marry him from a far country riding on a rich camel, sailing across the desert like a queen in a great ship."

After the breakdown following his ordination, a variety of physical sufferings afflicted him. He strained his back, broke into terrible allergic rashes, had one cold after another, constant influenza, sinus troubles—the Book of Job really spoke to him. He was, of course, writing again.

He had refused to be boxed in by his autobiography, and had consciously begun writing in a more spiritual, but no longer pietistic, style. He was misunderstood, and as his way of writing became more and more paradoxical, readers complained that what he said was contradictory.

"My life is almost totally paradoxical . . . I have become convinced that the very contradictions in my life are in some way signs of God's mercy to me: if only because someone so complicated and so prone to confusion and self-defeat could hardly survive for long without some special mercy."

Confusion characterized the reactions of many friends who had long predicted Tom's departure from the monastery. Now they told everyone it was just a matter of time until he left. Meanwhile, Tom was worried that all the public acclaim and the letters pouring in and the visitors beginning to come would make him a worse monk. But he was not a worse monk.

He was given yet one more job—he was elevated to the position of fire fighter for the monastery fire department.

"Merton was always the first out to fight a fire and the last to leave. He was a wild man with an ax," said John Howard Griffin.

And since he was always in the woods and loved the woods so much, he was also given another job—timber marker.

"I suddenly found out all about the trees. Next spring I shall presumably be in charge of planting ten thousand seedlings to replace what has been cut down. I started out with my pot of paint in October. The work began on the northeast flank of the lake knob . . . I have marked the trees in many different colors. . . ."

He was a monk who was a fire fighter and a tree-planter. That fit. In between times he dreamed of solitude. "I entertained for five minutes the reprehensible dream of building a hermitage."

He listened to the watch ticking on the table and the train whistling in the valley. The faint clanking of ropes against the metal flagpole in the garden filled him with nameless longing. Would he ever be given to live the life of a lonely, solitary contemplative? All the activity in which he was engaged made him ill in body, sardonic in mind. Yet the instant a period of silence and solitary prayer was granted him, no matter how brief, illness and worry fell away and he was filled with serene happiness.

One day, Father Cellarer permitted Tom to drive the jeep around the monastery, out of compassion for Tom's entrapment in so much activity.

It had been raining heavily. Tom had never driven a jeep. Nevertheless, he started out with great self-confidence, all by himself, taking off for the woods. Very soon he realized that he had never discovered the four-wheel drive. By this time, he had skidded into a ditch, ending up sideways in the middle of the road. A car was coming down the hill straight at him.

Later, he said: "Thank Heaven, I am still alive!"

But at the moment he didn't care a penny. He got the jeep under control and drove madly into the forest in a fog of delight, singing: "O Mary, I love you."

When he got back to the monastery, he and the jeep were covered with mud. He sneaked into choir at vespers, still high. "I have been driving a jeep!" he congratulated himself.

Father Cellarer, however, looked most unhappy. He fixed Tom with a fierce eye and made a sign that meant Father Louis must never, never under any circumstances, take the jeep out again—priest or no priest.

11

I tried to pray. . . . But the hawk was eating the bird.

As the fifties began, Thomas Merton thought more deeply than ever about his personal relation to the society of man, to the problems of war and peace, and to the struggle for racial justice which now, during this decade, began to surface and to break into the consciousness of Americans in general.

On June 22, 1951, he went to the Federal District Court, answered a lot of questions about his membership in socialist groups while at Columbia, and then he recited the oath of allegiance, received a flag from the Daughters of the American Revolution, and became a citizen.

In his journal, he wrote that for the first thirty-six years of his life he'd been proud of his freedom from national identity, thinking that by throwing away his earthly passport he would thereby become a citizen of heaven. Now he decided that the Naturalization Board, by making him a United States citizen, was actually helping him toward citizenship in the heavenly kingdom, simply because he now became a part of the human condition, by his own free will.

There was a grove of cedars, not yet cut down, just beyond

the east wall. Reverend Father gave him approval to have this woods as a refuge for his scholastics. They could learn as well, if not better, outdoors, walking in the woods. They worked, too, making firebreaks. The writer's hands were blistered. He would come back dirty and wringing wet to bathe and change his clothes. Then he would go sit alone under a tree behind the church to pray. But always the writing called him back to his desk. He burned with the inner compulsion to work even though he did not believe he was doing it to be "useful." His religious belief and the historical era in which he was placed came together to ignite him.

The mystics said God created man not to be useful, but for His delight, and Thomas Merton thought as the mystics did. When he became a priest, when he became a citizen, it was not so that he could be more useful. If God found Thomas Merton more delightful as a priest and a citizen, that was the way to go. He would never be an "activist priest" nor an activist citizen because of political or social theories, but—as Edward Rice said of his friend Tom Merton: "One doesn't always need a bomb or an underground to bring down the world: a word can do it, and the word was there, slowly altering the consciousness of man. . . ."

For Merton himself, the transformation of consciousness that led to his dual commitments as priest and citizen came through mysticism. Blake had said it all: "The transfiguration of man's natural love, his natural powers, in the refining fires of mystical experience."

It was after Thomas Merton was ordained a priest and then became a citizen that he began to pour forth his tremendous and fiery works on peace and racial justice, and to shock many who were religiously committed to the Church and did not think peace and racial justice and nonviolent resistance had anything to do with religion.

He was teaching his students and realizing anew that the Christian life—and especially the contemplative life—was a continual discovery of Christ in new and unexpected places. One such place was the South, where he was now rooted. He was a citizen of the United States, but he was also a Southerner.

Thomas Merton had often written of Christ's crucifixion,

seeing it as a metaphor for suffering. He had written of seeing Christ's crucifixion flowering in London, like a tree flowering in blood. He had written a fierce poem of Christ's crucifixion flowering in Harlem. Now he began writing of Christ's crucifixion flowering in the South. Soon he was writing of Christ as a great tree, the cosmic tree, bleeding from wounds like flowers all over America, all over Asia, and all over the world.

He did not have to go out of the monastery to learn about the unfolding history of his times. Visitors brought the news in, and so did letters. Southerners were the first to write to each other about the revolution that was happening—there had always been Southerners like William Faulkner, Lillian Smith, John Beecher, and John Howard Griffin, who were speaking out about racial justice long before the rest of the nation was aware.

In 1954, the United States Supreme Court, with Chief Justice Earl Warren at its head, heard a case entitled *Brown* v. *Board of Education*. The decision was in regard to a suit brought on behalf of a black child named Linda Brown who was denied entry into a public elementary school. The Supreme Court of the nation held that "separate but equal" justice was really an injustice because it was inherently unequal and therefore illegal.

Within a year another event took place in the South which began to rouse sensitive people not only in the South, but in the North, East, and West. A young black seamstress named Rosa Parks refused to give up her seat on a bus. If the bus was full, black people were supposed to give up their seats. A black person could not remain seated if a white person was standing, but Rosa Parks was tired, and she'd paid for her seat and wouldn't get up for a white man. The outraged bus driver stopped the bus and had her arrested.

A young minister just out of Boston University had recently arrived at his new pastorate in Montgomery, Alabama, with his young wife, Coretta. He had been greatly influenced by the writings of Mahatma Gandhi, just as Thomas Merton had. His name was Martin Luther King, Jr., and he began by preaching nonviolent resistance to evil as the essence of

Christianity. On the morning after the arrest of Rosa Parks—
it was a Friday morning, December 2, 1955—Martin Luther
King, Jr. got a telephone call from one of the civic leaders of
his community. As soon as he heard what had happened, he
called for a meeting of black ministers and community
leaders in his church. That night plans for a boycott were set
forth. All weekend he and his wife stayed up mimeographing
leaflets and making phone calls urging the bus boycott.

On Sunday night they could hardly sleep. Would any of
their people dare to support the boycott? Blacks had been
murdered for less. Monday morning, both Martin and
Coretta were up at dawn. Coretta ran to the front window to
wait for the first buses. Usually they would be carrying do-
mestic workers, who could lose their jobs for observing the
boycott. Suddenly she let out a yell: "Martin! Martin!"

He came running, coffee cup in hand. Empty buses!

"A miracle!" he whispered. The boycott was close to one
hundred percent effective, and thus the civil rights movement
was born, a movement not just for black freedom, but for
human justice.

All kinds of Americans were involved in this drama—old
people and young people, long-haired kids and priests with
no hair, rabbis and ministers, nuns and housewives. The
cause was for social justice. It was then that people began
marching.

Lillian Smith, a Southern writer long in the forefront of
those seeking racial justice, sent out copies of letters she had
received from those she called "the young and the brave"
who were joining the struggle. One of these letters said: "My
sister Priscilla and I, five other A & M students and one high
school student are serving 60-day sentences for our participation in the Sit-Ins. We could be out on appeal but we all
strongly believe that Martin Luther King was right when he
said, 'We've got to fill the jails in order to win our equal
rights.' Priscilla and I both explained this to our parents when
they visited us."

They came singing "We Shall Overcome" and carrying
their Bibles in their hands. Concerned citizens, seeing this,
demanded that the forces of law and order also carry Bibles
in their hands. But the lawmen had their hands full already

with tear-gas bombs, fire hoses, electric cattle prods, police dogs on chain-leashes. They had no room in their hands for their Bibles. And the freedom marchers went right on marching.

Thomas Merton began writing to the rhythm of the marchers, praying and writing with so much force that Martin Luther King, Jr. said: "Merely to have someone like Merton take our side would have been enough, but we could not have asked for a more effective statement of the case."

From his unique vantage point as a writer who was a monk in the oldest and most traditional Judeo-Christian establishment, the Roman Catholic Church, Thomas Merton helped introduce the twentieth-century "counter culture" and nonviolent resistance to the bourgeois society as basic Christianity.

"The publication of *The Seven Storey Mountain* and its runaway success established him in the seemingly contradictory status of a 'Trappist celebrity.' The subsequent decision, wise as it was unusual, to permit him, even encourage him, to pursue his literary career and maintain the outside contacts this would involve and require, was to provide him with the public platform from which he could voice his prophetic message," writes Gordon Zahn, the great Catholic pacifist.

After *The Seven Storey Mountain* became a best seller, it was natural that readers all over the world would listen and be alert whenever Thomas Merton had anything to say. It turned out that he had plenty to say. His life of prayer and contemplation was not separated from human concerns: the bomb dropped on Hiroshima, the peace marchers, and the struggle for racial justice. All of this was Satyagraha or Truth Force. Meditation led to Truth; Truth was a Force.

He was as committed to the cause of freedom, justice, and nonviolent resistance of evil in Russia, as in the United States. In the essay he wrote on Boris Pasternak, he said:

"If Pasternak is ever fully studied, he is just as likely to be regarded as a dangerous writer in the West as he is in the East. He is saying that political and social structures as we understand them are things of the past, and the crisis through which we are now passing is nothing but the manifestation of their falsity. For twenty centuries we have called ourselves Christians, without even beginning to understand one tenth of the Gospel."

In his own way, he too was marching with the marchers. He was writing at a furious pace about everything that was exploding in the history of his times, and simultaneously he was writing about theology, prayer, meditation, and his studies which were leading him deeper and deeper into Zen Buddhist research. With the sardonic humor he could always turn on himself as well as on others, he noted that while some men lead lives that cry out to heaven for vengeance and persecution and others suffer the persecution, he, meanwhile, writes books.

But the books he wrote spoke the word, and the word was the catalyst that helped make the action a movement toward significant goals, rather than a chaotic movement of frustrated individuals.

In the choir the young monks listened and discussed the fascinating ways in which contemplation led to action. Merton would look at them with compassion. "The young monks, patient, serene, with very clear eyes . . . gentle, confused. For years I have given them classes. Thus they become more confused."

But he wanted them to be aware, as well as religious, to think more deeply and to question their own complacencies. The life of physical labor had to go on, right along with the writing and the praying and the teaching. He took the scholastics out to plant trees. They put in thousands of seedlings in the places that had been logged, yellow poplar and loblolly pine and other trees. And he still arose each day at 2:15 A.M. to pray, to walk outside and have the dawn to himself.

"I have almost two hours to pray or read or think by myself and make up the Night Office. I am all alone in the cool world of morning. . . ."

At 2:15 A.M. the young bulls were still asleep behind their electric fence. He thought of the importance of nature for contemplation. A friend, Paul Sih, had obtained for him a wonderful reprint of the James Legge translation of the Chinese classics.

Manual labor and the work of prayer and meditation and

the work of writing went together—they made each other better.

But he was doing too much. "I have a huge mass of half-digested notes, all mixed up." Sometimes he felt he could not sort it all out. Somebody told him of a Carthusian monk who suffered from "sacred exhaustion." Father Louis took to the phrase: "I experience it from head to foot," he said with a self-deprecatory smile.

He was writing for the marchers and the students and also for those who had made a religious commitment. He wanted to explain the vocabulary of the counter culture as the exact language of Christianity, so that all Christians would recognize nonviolent resistance to evil as the heart of theology as set forth by Christ.

"For the Hindu, the solid metaphysical and religious basis was provided by the Vedantist doctrine of the Atman. . . . For the Christian the basis of nonviolence is the Gospel message. . . ."

Many people believed that the struggle for peace and racial justice was not just a crisis of Western civilization. They believed this was the end of the world and that, as predicted, humanity was sinking under the waves of hatred and guilt. Thomas Merton's students were interested in the discussions he led on eschatology—the theological word for the doctrine of final things, like the Last Judgment. They, too, like everyone else, were caught up in predictions and prophecies.

It was a time of end-of-the-world threats. Some prophesied the end from words in the Bible, decoding passages of scripture to predict doom. Others prophesied from ancient Egyptian writings and from the pyramids. There were Black Muslims prophesying that Mother Plane would drop hundreds of "eggs" to blast the world to death. There were Catholics prophesying from Fatima (where the Virgin appeared to children in Portugal at the time of the Russian Revolution and the close of World War I) that unless Communism was overthrown and Russia was converted, the end was coming. But Father Louis Merton said: "The time of the end is the time of no room." That's what eschatology was all about —it was about an inner-space war, not an outer-space war. His

ooked confused, so he tried to explain the symbol
om." When Christ entered human history there was
for Him in the affairs of humanity, and the symbol
inn that had no room. A bit later the idea was
t in the story of the Good Samaritan, where a per-
gged, beaten up and left for dead, and everybody
too busy to stop and give a care, except one outcast
aritan, an alien in the land. This person alone
e in his life to help somebody who was hurt. So it
t up to the present moment, and still there was no
"Christ-love." No room was "the time of the end"
n the beginning. ←

l eschatology must not be confused with the vague
us eschatology of human foreboding," he told his

as if he were talking too much. Yet all the time,
ts were getting more than he imagined. They could
being confused, for they had been told so many
ut the doom at the end, about the apparitions, the
Every Mass ended with prayers for the "Conversion of Russia" as if nobody else in the world needed prayers
to be converted. Get rid of Communism and the catastrophic
end would be averted.

Now here was Father Louis, their teacher, telling them
that this was a pathological fear, and that such fears were really a thinly disguised hope for violence, a hope for a violent
end, in opposition to the truth force of eschatology.

He read to them from *The Book of the Apocalypse*, the es-
chatological book of books, which describes the "Saints and
Martyrs, Priests and Witnesses" biding their time, "loving
one another and the truth" in lives of gentleness and
"meekness, patience, poverty." They did not live in perpetual
fear that the violent would bear it away.

Were his students getting the idea? Was the theology of
love coming through?

"I am throwing myself too much into this classwork. That
is one thing that is wearing me down. . . . There is no need
to try to sweep them off their feet by sheer intensity."

Teaching and learning went together—the Bible and the
study of Zen, the great Eastern mystics and the great West-

ern mystics, such as Julian of Norwich, whom Merton particularly loved.

Julian of Norwich also spoke of the end. She said that the end of time was not a triumph of hate, but a triumph of love —"not a deed of destruction and revenge, but of mercy and life." And, she said, it was already accomplished through the coming of Christ—everything that was to be accomplished through Him was already accomplished. All was well.

All was well at the end of time. But while time was, all was not well, and the work to be done had to be clear. Merton clarified. He spoke to his students about the difference between Truth and Expedience, and read them an illustration. It was from a letter of Topf and Sons, manufacturers of heating equipment, to the Commandant of Auschwitz: "We acknowledge the receipt of your order for five triple furnaces including two electric elevators for raising the corpses and one emergency elevator." The Commandant, elated with the efficiency of Topf and Sons, bragged that his camp had achieved the ultimate in expediency—over Treblinka and all the other death camps: "Our gas chambers . . . accommodate 2,000 people at a time, whereas at Treblinka their gas chambers only accommodated 200 people each."

One afternoon Tom went up to the attic of the gardenhouse and stood among the broken strawberry boxes, looking out of the small window. The sky was overcast. Streamers of sunlight came through the clouds like a shining fan. In the trees the starlings chirped and hopped; then a hawk swooped down. The starlings rose out of the trees like a cloud, came to earth for an instant, then winged away. But one did not make it. The hawk dived and nailed him.

The silence was intense. Not a bird in sight, not a sound, only the starling under the talon of the hawk, and the hawk eating.

"I tried to pray but the hawk was eating the bird." Tom could not pull his eyes away. There was the contradiction of beauty in the kill; the hawk's unerring skill had been beautiful. He had to transpose the hawk's skill upward, to make it a spiritual metaphor; so he began to pray that he serve his God as unerringly as the hawk served its nature. "My heart stirred to serve Christ, as you, soldier, serve your nature. And God's love a thousand times more terrible!"

The fifties were years that unfolded surprises, one after another. Not the least of these surprises was Pope John XXIII, the new pope whose coronation in November of 1958 brought to a climax the seeming test of the Judeo-Christian ideal.

Almost at once Pope John announced the "opening of the church." The Church was to open itself to society. He spoke of society as the kingdom of man: "What are kingdoms without justice but large bands of robbers?" The poor and oppressed peoples everywhere were asking exactly the same question, and, just a few years later, Pope John, in his peace encyclical, *Pacem in Terris*, offered some answers. The waves that Pope John made were tidal, and many warned he was endangering the Church. He himself had troubled dreams and would wake up, saying to himself: "I must go and ask the pope what to do about this." Then he realized: "But I am the pope!"

Father Louis Merton had the same Christian ideas about peace as Pope John, and he, too, felt he had nobody to ask for answers. There were no more authoritative answers. The new pope believed, as did Thomas Merton and many others, that this particular era was profoundly significant. The entire human race seemed involved in a vast upheaval.

"Christianity and the world: this is a matter about which suddenly one must have an approved answer. I have none."

But not having "approved answers" did not stop Thomas Merton from writing. The fact that he had no answers seemed to make him write all the more. He was writing a lot about Pope John XXIII now, and Pope John sent Merton the stole he had worn at his coronation as a signal gift of love.

A Tibetan student stopped by the monastery to visit Thomas Merton and Merton asked him about the Tibetan monks. The student said the Dalai Lama was very anxious to have the monks that were with him in India trained in the knowledge of Western culture and religion.

It was strangely like Merton's own ideas. He was very anxious that monks who were trained in the knowledge of Western culture and religion become aware of Eastern culture and religion. He was writing on these themes more and more now. Until very recently, writings even by Christian mystics were regarded with suspicion in Catholic monasteries. As for Oriental mysticism, it was even more a "hands-off" subject. Now, all of this had changed, thanks to the opening up of the Church. Far from being suspicious of the Oriental mystical traditions, Catholic contemplatives were encouraged to study the centuries-old translations the first Jesuit missionaries had made of Taoist scriptures.

"It takes more than study to penetrate Zen," wrote Merton. But he was ready. The paradoxes of the Zen mystics were akin to his own nature. When he read:

"The doors and windows are cut out [from the walls] to form an apartment; but it is on the empty space [within] that its use depends" he understood the Tao and its stress on the use of what seems useless. He went at once and offered Mass for the new generation, the fighters for peace and civil rights, whom he called the new poets, and for his novices who were going to have to live in empty spaces.

The new poets, his novices, and the fighters for peace and civil rights, were the poles turning the spiritual axis, and Fr. Merton was at the center generating the love force. His writings on war and peace, violence and nonviolence, Satyagraha (Truth Force) were appearing, often in the form of letters in Dorothy Day's *Catholic Worker*. These essays had a stirring effect on the young. It was the end of the fifties, just at the turn of the mid-twentieth century. The sixties became the testing point for a change in mentality. The peace and human rights movements were testing the words of Christianity that had been spoken for so many centuries.

The young generations coming to maturity in the sixties turned to Thomas Merton. They did not turn to him as their leader, for *they* were the leaders. Indeed, Merton rebuffed all ideas of leadership for himself. But he was pleased to be their spiritual guide, the Christian mystic, monk, and contemplative who could give them the impetus of religious clarification which they needed. They did not know that this was how he regarded his role, or not at first. They were simply looking for backing from Christians, assuming that they—obviously—knew what Christ's words put-into-action signified.

But "respectable" Christians, including Catholics—to whom Fr. Merton was a vital spiritual guide opening vistas of contemplative prayer—did not identify the call to serve Christ in pacifist or racial justice, as the logical consequence of Christ's teachings. Just the opposite. Many felt Fr. Merton was getting into "politics," which was wrong. They felt bitterly betrayed, to such an extent that some of those who had been most devoted to his writings and stimulating spirituality became heavily involved in spreading extraordinary, false, and malicious rumors. (In later years, as history unfolded, these rumors were said to have been started by the FBI, much as in the case of the Baptist minister, Martin Luther King, Jr., to destroy the credibility of such pacifist and racial justice "agitators"—in the interests of national security.)

The censors of Merton's order sought to tone him down. But the young people were inspired. One Christmas, just as the nineteen-sixties were beginning, Merton invited any members of the *Catholic Worker* staff who were free to come to Gethsemani for a few days. James Forest and Bob Kaye accepted. Later James Forest would be well-known as a leader in the Fellowship of Reconciliation, in the United States and internationally.

They all took to each other immediately and became strong friends. The young men wanted to talk about the attitude of the Church, still clinging to the nineteenth-century tradition of the "just war." Merton said that somewhere in the last fifty years we have crossed a mysterious limit—"we have passed a point of no return, and it is both useless and tragic to continue to live as if we were still in the nineteenth century." But essays were appearing in prestigious Catholic journals challenging the pacifists. The essayists spoke as Christian writers who saw the need to save the Christian faith from communism. Father Merton declared: "The big question is indeed to save the Christian faith, but if we strive to save it with bombs and nuclear submarines we are going to lose it." He admitted that he was not a total pacifist. "But what I do assert is that the Church, the clergy, the Catholic lay apostles, the Catholic teacher, the Catholic intellectual have a serious obligation today to investigate the meaning and the feasability of nonviolent defense not only on the individual but on the national level." He was not denying a man the right to defend himself and his children, but there was no longer a tenable argument for a "just war" in an age of nuclear and atomic weapons.

They walked in the snowy woods, discussing the way the Church *sees*, "not just from the viewpoint of natural ethics." They spoke of the Mass and how this sacrifice represented the whole connection. And they sat in class with the novices to listen to Merton teach. When they said good-by, they gave Merton a peace button and he pinned it on his robes.

It was the beginning of an impassioned involvement with those out on the streets in the city and in the country. His aim was pastoral. He was the missionary to the peace activists, on the outside, and to the religious contemplatives, on the inside. Many both outside and inside did not get the point. They thought they should teach him. Many of the peace activists had no idea what he was talking about. They had rarely if ever heard the beatitudes, the gospels, religion, taught as a work of the spirit made flesh. But patiently, in his writings, letters, and essays (which even when "censored" passed from hand to hand), he went on explaining and enlightening. He insisted on opening the minds of the pacifists to the religious dimension basic to any peace movement: "Without the religious dimension even pacifism and nonviolence are relatively meaningless." He repeated over and over that nonviolence does not make sense "if one does not also have faith in God. This, of course, complicates matters tremendously because of the scandal that so many who claim to believe in God, enlist Him in their wars. God is always the first one to be drafted, and this is a universal stumbling block."

Many of the Movement People were baffled when he spoke of such things as "purity" in their nonviolent action, and detachment from results and said that: "We must act only because the act itself is true and expresses the truth . . . as for results: truth needs only to be manifested. It can take care of itself." But their bafflement was no greater than that of some of the religious who also did not understand when he compared the monks at prayer to atom bombs. The monks were bombs stored in silos—as death bombs were stored in silos, so monks were life-bombs stored in silos. "These are the monks of the twentieth century: the fellows cloistered in the bomb silo, with their communal life, their silence, their austerity, their separation from the world." They dug into the earth to find the sources of life as the bombs of death dug into the earth with the power of death.

He told them (the contemplatives): "Whatever I may have written, I think it can all be reduced in the end to this one root truth: that God calls human persons to union with Himself and with one another in Christ, in the Church, which is his Mystical Body. It is also a witness to the fact that there is, and must be, in the Church a contemplative life which has no other function than to realize these mysterious things, and return to God all the thanks and praise that human hearts can give Him."

This was why prayer was of the essence, and becoming a hermit was of the essence. All had to go together.

12

*Last night I had a curious dream about
Kanchenjunga. . . . And I heard a voice saying. . . .
'There is another side to the mountain.'*

"On my forty-sixth birthday they put an ape into space."
Thomas Merton thought it was a fantastically apt way to
commemorate the date. There were also 106 nuclear tests
that year—1961.

Father Louis Merton felt that it was now the acceptable
time to "filter a little Zen into our lives." In 1960 he had
translated *The Ox Mountain Parable* of Meng Tzu, noting
that the period, the 4th and 3rd century B.C., was an age of
war and chaos like ours.

The parable told of a fine forest once growing on Ox
Mountain. Men came with axes and cut down the trees.
Then, resting in the alternation of days and nights, mois-
tened by dew, the stumps sprouted, the trees began to grow
again. Out came goats and cattle to browse on the young
shoots. Ox Mountain was stripped utterly bare. The people,
seeing it stripped utterly bare think Ox Mountain never had
any woods on it at all.

"Our mind too, stripped bare, like the mountain,
 Still cannot be without some basic tendency to love."

But, as men with axes cutting down the trees every morning destroy the beauty of the forest, so we by our daily actions destroy our right minds. Yet God renews the mind again—night comes giving rest to the murdered forest, and night is followed by "the dawn spirit" awakening in us the right loves, "the right aversions."

He was writing many articles on classic Chinese thought. Besides translating *The Ox Mountain Parable*, he wrote *The Way of Chuang Tzu*, which he liked best of all his books. He was also engaged in dialogue with Daisetz T. Suzuki. When Dr. Suzuki came to New York in 1961, he asked Merton to come and see him since he was unable to go to the abbey. Permission was given, and, on the day arranged, Thomas Merton returned to the great city he had left so many years ago.

Suzuki was ninety-four years old, a thin old man, deaf, yet sharply aware and lively, giving the impression of an immortal. They drank green tea out of dark brown bowls and talked of Zen. Suzuki read Father Louis some stories from a Chinese text, and Merton read Suzuki from some Spanish translations and from the English mystics. One phrase, from one of the things Merton was reading, made Suzuki exclaim with joy. The phrase was: "Praise be to God that I am not good!" Suzuki applauded. "That is so important!"

Back at the monastery, it was blazing hot, and Merton thought of the heat in New York and the summer rain on rainy streets under rainy trees. New York was anything but soulless. She was a great lady, a great city. "I have not ceased to love her," he said. "I am faithful to her."

The great city brought home to him, sharply, the awareness of being a bystander. He was writing a book called *Conjectures of a Guilty Bystander*. He called it a personal version of the world in the 1960s.

The decade following the 1950s brought to ripeness a fearful fruit—assassinations and the Vietnam War. A whole generation of young people rejected a world they never made, and turned instead to drugs, seeking a more transcendent plane of existence. In the light of new experiments with chemical short-cuts to transcendence, it seemed possible.

Aldous Huxley had written in the fifties about his experiments with mescaline. His book, *The Doors of Perception*, became more and more popular each year, and many of the young took up the idea of "better living through chemistry."

It was curious that the same writer who had so inspired young Thomas Merton could still inspire a whole new generation to seek for some way out of a spiritually closed universe. Thomas Merton decided to write a long letter to Huxley, asking about the experiments with mescaline and other such drugs. He wanted to know if the experiences Huxley reported were not more in the realm of heightened aesthetic experiences rather than experiences of union with God. Huxley responded with a long letter. He defended the use of consciousness-raising drugs, but only for those who were already prepared with in-depth studies of mysticism. In his own case he said that Christian mystics, like Julian of Norwich and Francis of Assisi, were as vital to his sources of mystical knowledge as the Buddhist mystics. He wished to impress on "Father Merton" that under no circumstances were experiments "so transcendently important" to be entered just for the sake of sensation, or "taking drugs."

Merton, as one who had ventured his total existence on the discipline of prayer, was a religious mystic and his great concern was to clarify the difference between mysticism as a state of the soul (and mind), arrived at via disciplines of prayer, and mysticism as an experiment in sensory experience, arrived at through chemistry. In his letter to Aldous Huxley dated November 27, 1958, Merton after expressing his faithful remembrance of and affection for Huxley, who had been spiritually stimulating to his own youth, sought to engage the older writer in dialogue. He wrote:

Dear Mr. Huxley:

Twenty years, or nearly that many, have gone by since a very pleasant exchange of letters took place between us. The other day, in correcting the proofs of a Journal I kept then, and which is being published now, I was reminded of the fact. I shall send you the book when it appears. The final entries, in which you are mentioned,

will testify to the gratitude and friendship with which I
have continued to remember you since then.

Meanwhile I am happy to open another discussion
with you, and I intend to do so in a spirit which will, I
hope, lead to something quite constructive. For I assure
you that I have no wish whatever to enter into a silly argument, and that I approach you with none of the
crudities or prejudices which I am sure annoy you in
other clerics. I do not, of course, claim to be above the
ordinary human failings of religious people, but I think I
am at least relatively free of partisanship and fanaticism.

Your article in the *Saturday Evening Post* on drugs
that help man achieve an experience of self-transcend-
ence, has, you know, created quite a stir. We do not
read the *Saturday Evening Post* here in the monastery,
but a good lady sent me a copy of your article, together
with a copy of a letter she sent you advising you to read
Fr. Garrigou Lagrange on contemplation. May God pre-
serve you from such a fate.

I am in no position to dispute what you say about the
effect of drugs. Though occasionally fortified by aspirin,
and exhilarated by coffee, and even sometimes using a
barbiturate to get to sleep (alas), I have no experience
of the things you speak of. Perhaps I shall make a trial
of them one of these days, so that I will know what I
am talking about. But since I feel, as you do, that this is
a matter which merits discussion and study, I would like
to put forward the things that occur to me after my first
encounter with the subject. I hope by this to *learn*
rather than to teach, and I can see that this is your attitude also. Therefore, if you will permit me, I would like
to take up the implicit invitation you expressed in the
article, and invite you still further, if you are interested,
to go into this with us. If you are ever in this neigh-
borhood perhaps you could come here and we could talk
at leisure. Our mutual friends, Victor Hammer and his
wife at Lexington would gladly bring you over.

After this preamble, here are the questions I would
like to raise:

1) Are you not endangering the whole concept of gen-

uine mystical experience in saying that it is something that can be "produced" by a drug? I know, you qualify the statement, you say that a drug can induce a state in which mystical experience can be occasioned: a drug can remove obstacles in our ordinary everyday state of mind, and make a kind of latent mysticism come to the surface. But I wonder if this accords with the real nature of mystical experience?

I think this point must be studied rather carefully, and I suggest the following:

2) Ought we not to distinguish between an experience which is essentially *aesthetic and natural* from an experience which is *mystical and supernatural*. I would call aesthetic and natural an experience which would be an intuitive "tasting" of the inner spirituality of our own being—or an intuition of being as such, arrived at through an intuitive awareness of our own inmost reality. This would be an experience of "oneness" within oneself and with all beings, a flash of awareness of the transcendent Reality that is within all that is real. This sort of thing "happens" to one in all sorts of ways, and I see no reason why it should not be occasioned by the use of a drug. This intuition is very like the aesthetic intuition that precedes the creation of a work of art. It is like the intuition of a philosopher who rises above the concepts and their synthesis to see everything in one glance, in all its length, height, breadth, and depth. It is like the intuition of a person who has participated deeply in a liturgical act. (I think you take too cavalier an attitude toward liturgy, although I confess that I am irked by liturgical enthusiasts when they want to regiment others into their way of thinking.) By the way, though I call this experience "natural" that does not preclude its being produced by the action of God's grace (a term that must be used with care). But I mean that it is not in its mode or in its content beyond the capacities of human nature itself. Please forgive me for glibly using this distinction between natural and supernatural as if I were quite sure where the dividing line came. Of course I am not.

What would I call a *supernatural and mystical* experience then? I speak very hesitantly, and do not claim to be an authority. What I say may be very misleading. It may be the product of subjective and sentimental illusion, or it may be the product of a rationalization superimposed on the experience described above. Anyway, here goes.

It seems to me that a fully mystical experience has in its very essence some note of a direct spiritual *contact of two liberties,* a kind of a flash or spark which ignites an intuition of all that has been said above, *plus* something much more which I can only describe as "personal," in which God is known not as an "object" or as "in up there" or "Him in everything" or as "the All" but as— the Biblical expression—I AM, or simply AM. But what I mean is that this is not the kind of intuition that smacks of anything procurable because it is a presence of a Person and *depends on the liberty of that Person.* And lacking the element of free gift, a free act of love on the part of Him Who comes, the experience would lose its specifically mystical quality.

3) But now, from the moment that such an experience can be conceived as *dependent on* and *inevitably following from* the casual use of a material instrument, it loses the quality of spontaneity and freedom and transcendence which makes it truly mystical.

This is my main question. It seems to me that for this reason, expressed lamely perhaps and without full understanding, real mystical experience would be more or less incompatible with the *consistent* use of a drug.

Here are some further thoughts.

Supposing a person with a genuine vocation to mystical union. And supposing that person starts to use a drug. And supposing further that I am correct in the above estimate of what real mystical experience consists in: then—the one using the drug can produce what I have called a "natural and aesthetic" experience. But at the same time his higher "conscience" (here I mean not merely a moral censor, but his inmost spirit in its function of "judge" between what is real and what isn't) will inevitably reproach him for self-delusion. He will enjoy the experience for a moment, but it will be followed not by the inner permanent strengthening of a real spiritual experience, but by lassitude, discouragement, confusion, *and an increased need for the drug*. This will produce a vicious circle of repeated use of the drug, renewed lassitude and guilt, greater need for the drug, and final complete addiction with the complete ruin of a mystical vocation, if not worse.

What I say here is based on suppositions, of course. I do not attempt to impose the analysis on you, but I would be very interested in your judgment of what I have said and your opinion in the matter.

I will not weary you by prolonging this letter, but will close here in the hope that we can go further into the matter later on.

May I add that I am interested in Yoga and above all in Zen, which I find to be the finest example of a technique leading to the highest *natural* perfection of man's contemplative liberty. You may argue that use of a Koan to dispose one for Satori is no different from the use of a drug. I would like to submit that there is all the difference in the world, and perhaps we can speak more of this later. My dear Mr. Huxley, it is a joy to write to you of these things. I hope you can reply. God bless you. With warm affection in Christ.

(Thomas Merton)

Aldous Huxley's long letter described his participation in scientific experiments with mescaline and lysergic acid. He defended the researchers and clinicians, including himself, working in this area, and said the work was "profoundly significant." Yet he agreed with Merton's criticism that the states described in these experiments could be "mainly aesthetic." But he said that in his own case, "later experiences were of another nature." His letter ended by emphasizing that "the experience is so transcendently important that it is in no circumstances a thing to be entered upon light-heartedly or for enjoyment." And he declared that those who embark on this route are also under intellectual disciplines which must keep them from "repeating the experiment at frequent intervals." Indeed, they are expected to "go on from there" to use the spiritual technique of mystics like the fourteenth-century Christian, Eckhart—one of Huxley's favorite Christian mystics. Eckhart's route to transcendent experience, however, was the identical one pursued and taught by Merton; i.e., through prayer, penance, and poverty of material things.

Huxley indeed opposed the use of drugs by uninformed, uneducated, undisciplined, and intellectually and spiritually unprepared people. And when, in 1955, CBS invited him to participate in a series of television shows, he declined. He wrote his friend, Dr. Humphry Osmond: "Mescaline, it seems to me, and the odder aspects of mind are matters to be written about for a small public, not discussed on TV in the presence of a vast audience." He said: "We still know very little about the psychedelics, and until we know a good deal more, I think the matter should be discussed, and the investigations described, in the relative privacy of learned journals, the decent obscurity of moderately high-brow books and articles."

In a way, this exchange of ideas on chemical mysticism was just as important to Thomas Merton as the exchange with D. T. Suzuki on Zen. Tom was always seeking to know more. But there was also his anxiety that the young should find authentic spirituality. The young were in the streets; they were out in huge numbers, marching and creating frightening images. Some people speculated that these young marchers with their strange looks, their long hair and fanatical eyes, were really the ghost dancers prophesied by the American Indians who had been slaughtered to make way for this new nation.

Along with everything else he was writing, Thomas Merton was also writing about "The Ghost Dance Movement" which originated among the Paviotso Indians near Walker Lake, Nevada, about 1869. This was a religious movement which anticipated the return of the Indians who had died in battle. But now not just the Indians but *all* the young who had died in battle were rising up out of their graves. They were coming back, all the young who had been defrauded of their lives: "they were all coming with cups in their hands to drink from

. . . all coming in a group. No distinction would exist any more between races."

People feared the long-haired boys and girls filling the streets and highways of the nation. There were no distinctions in sex, just as St. Paul had prophesied, "there was neither Jew nor Greek, nor male nor female." They had been deprived of the right to live their lives; they had died too young, and they were the ghost dancers, reincarnated in the long-haired people who were marching all over the nation. They were back from the wars, all with long hair because hair grows long in the grave.

As the world of the 1960s entered into his consciousness, Thomas Merton responded with further writings on peace, truth, and the purpose of contemplation. It was not long before he got into trouble with conservative Christians. Certain authorities in his own order said he was talking too much. His censor put a ban on his book *Peace in the Post Christian Era*. He accepted the ban—in obedience—but kept right on writing more fiery peace essays. He didn't fight the censor, he just mimeographed all the most denunciatory chapters, especially those against the Vietnam War as well as against war in general, and sent them all over the world in mimeographed form. What did he care about publication? The word went out, one way or another.

Then one day a letter came from Rome assuring Father Louis that his new book, *Seeds of Destruction*, was to be passed by the censor without change. This book contained most of what he had written in his banned book, *Peace in the Post Christian Era*. So the "forbidden material" was published. The very thing the censor did not want to happen, happened. Yet Thomas Merton had remained steadfast to his vow of obedience the whole time. When the right to publish came, it was brought about without a single act on his own initiative. He had been content to accept the censor's ban, in obedience, and go on writing and sending his works all over the world, just like any "silenced" poet in Russia who nevertheless had his works circulating everywhere through the underground press.

In the midst of all this Merton along with Pope John

XXIII received a Peace prize, the Pax Medal. "Me and Pope John," he said, and wrote the Abbot General, humorously: "It is a good thing Pope John didn't have to get his encyclical through our censors." No bitterness, just humor.

Merton saw the inner landscape, the spiritual sea, the ebb and flow of prayer. He said that marching for peace was also prayer and he was praying with their marching. Writing his poem "Original Child Bomb," he was reprimanded by a superior, who said: "It is not your place to write about nuclear war; that is for the bishops."

Because of his passionate involvement with the world through his continuing writings on peace and justice while at the same time being a monk, many people were confused about Thomas Merton. Some explained that he was leaving the church; others that he had married. Some even said he had committed suicide. Letters filled with hate sometimes came from those who found his writings a threat.

At the opposite end were the ones who were exasperated with this monk because he wouldn't jump on their bandwagon. He was one with those who sought radical change in the Church, but he did not think that meant changing ancient and noble traditions in music, literature, history, and scripture. He saw change as consciousness-raising. He sought to liberate monastic and religious life from the deadening shell of its trivial and superficial elements.

During Pentecost, June 1963, Pope John XXIII died. Merton said that Pope John had done more in four years to knock down walls separating people from each other than anyone had for centuries.

"He was deeply concerned with the humanity which he shared with his fellow man. *Pacem in Terris* is not theology. It simply says that war is a sin because it is *inhuman*. . . . May he rest in peace, this great good Father whom I certainly loved, who had been personally very kind to me. I do not think he has stopped being a father to us and to me. If we last long enough, we will canonize him. I do not hesitate to ask his intercession now."

As usual, Thomas Merton could not run with the pack. "For my own part, I consider myself neither an extreme conservative nor an extreme progressive. I would like to think I am what Pope John was—a progressive with a deep respect and love for tradition."

But if he had to choose, he would choose the extreme progressives over the reactionaries because the reactionaries were fanatically incoherent, and he never sensed in the extreme progressives "the chilling malice and meanness which comes through in some of the utterances of extreme conservatives."

Buddhist monks told Thomas Merton that the same conflicts were going on in Buddhism. These stresses and strains within his own communion gave Father Louis a deeper comprehension of Buddhist renewal.

"This new Buddhism is not immersed in an eternal trance. Nor is it engaged in a fanatical self-glorifying quest for political power. It is not remote and withdrawn from the sufferings of ordinary men and their problems in a world of revolution. It seeks to help them. . . ."

In Hattiesburg, Mississippi, the Rosary Roman Catholic Church was bombed. Three college students who had gone into Mississippi to register black people to vote disappeared.

"I hear the bodies of the three young civil rights workers murdered in Mississippi in June have been strangely found, in an earth dam," Merton wrote. They had been tortured and their bodies mutilated. It was as if the harvest of these years was never going to end; the bad fruit kept ripening.

Coming down from the woods on an afternoon in late November he saw one of the novices holding open the door of the novitiate and calling "Father Louis" in a tragic voice. As he came up to the door the novice told him that President Kennedy had been shot and had died in Dallas, Texas, a couple of hours earlier.

Merton felt sick at heart. Later he wrote to his close friend, Jacques Maritain, telling him the horror everyone felt.

"I have never experienced such a thing as the spiritual crisis into which the violent death of President Kennedy has thrown the entire nation . . . it is almost an apocalyptic event, a revelation of most powerful forces of evil . . . a kind of spiritual cancer at work (in the very heart of the nation) . . . the frank and cynical rejoicing . . . among the racists."

Father Louis went late at night to stand in the empty novitiate, thinking of his students, the young monks. Their love and their goodness filled the room with a comforting presence.

How often had he renounced forever his dream of a hermitage, accepting the order's rebuffs! "God will prepare for me His own hermitage for my last days, and meanwhile my work is my hermitage . . . writing helps me most of all to be a solitary and a contemplative here at Gethsemani."

Then, suddenly, after all his renouncing of the hermit life, the gift of the hermitage came. A cinderblock cabin had been built, at Merton's suggestion, on a wooded hill about a mile from the monastery. There he could meet for purposes of ecumenical dialogue with the leaders of various faiths. At a meeting of Cistercian abbots of North and South America, in October 1964, Merton had suggested that the abbots consider the creation of hermitages, to be attached to monasteries, for those called to the solitary life. Out of his own deepest needs since his first days as a monk, he came to make this very personal, original (for the twentieth century) contribution to the quest for God.

Afterward, the Abbot General wrote a letter to Dom James saying he was not opposed in principle to experiments in the hermit life within the Trappist order, and that such an experiment at Gethsemani was feasible and even reasonable. Thomas Merton had changed the order!

Slightly less than a year after the meeting of the abbots, he received permission to live in the hermitage day and night, permanently. He lived alone, but came down to the monastery for his dinner, and to give talks in "Chapter" on Sunday afternoons. Friends visited him on special occasions. In a letter dated August 17, 1965, he wrote to Sister M. Therese Lentfoehr, one of his closest friends—he'd known her for twenty years, and she typed many of his manuscripts.

"This week I officially begin the hermit life. . . . It is quite a step, and something that has not been done thus officially in the Order since the Lord knows when, way back in the Middle Ages, when we had a few hermit saints. I hope I will follow in their footsteps (sanely however)."

When he wrote that he hoped to follow in the footsteps of

the hermit saints "sanely," he knew what he was talking about. He learned, those first days and nights, that solitude meant that the ropes were cast off, the ship was no longer tied to land but headed out to sea: "not the sea of passion, on the contrary, the sea of purity and love that is without care, that loves God alone immediately and directly in Himself, as the All, and the seeming Nothing that is All."

Solitude was dangerous. Just sitting didn't suffice, you must pray or else go to seed. A chill sometimes came up and breathed on the back of his neck. He felt the dank cold of the void that is without breath, airless. "Where does this naked and cold darkness come from?" he asked. What did the sudden chill mean, did it mean death? Who are you when you do not exist? Perhaps the answer to that was knowing who you are when you do exist.

"In the hermitage I see how quickly one can fall apart. I talk to myself, I dance around the hermitage, I sing. This is all very well, but it is not serious, it is a manifestation of weakness."

Or of strength! The spirit of God was essentially joy, was play, or, as Merton quoted from Chuang Tzu, the awareness that nothing is more useless than the useful and what is really useful is the useless. Thomas Merton put the whole idea into a signed confession, attesting to the overpowering uselessness of pure joy.

"I confess that I am sitting under a pine tree doing absolutely nothing. I have done nothing for one hour and firmly intend to continue to do nothing for an indefinite period . . . I have taken my shoes off. I confess that I have been listening to a mockingbird . . . I confess furthermore that there is a tanager around here somewhere. . . ."

Before he became a hermit, he sometimes told himself that he probably would find hermitage life nothing like what he imagined. Now he was learning that it was all he had imagined and more, and that everything the early fathers had said about the solitary life was true, including the temptations as well as the joys, and "above all the tears and the incredible peace and happiness . . . happiness . . . so pure because it is simply not one's own making, but sheer mercy and gift. . . ."

The hermitage was perfect—spiritually. The things that could have been more perfect included running water—there was none, no running water, no electricity, no bathroom. Going out to the privy when the temperature was zero or below could be a grievous shock. Even so, crunching over the snow and the dried corn husks laid down to keep feet from slipping, you could look into the night sky where a thin slice of leftover moon clung.

All was well, as Julian of Norwich had said. He was reading her all the time. "Julian of Norwich is without doubt one of the most wonderful of all Christian voices . . . I think that Julian of Norwich is with Newman the greatest Catholic theologian. She is really that. . . . I used to be crazy about St. John of the Cross. I would not exchange him now for Julian if you gave me the world and the Indies and all the Spanish mystics rolled up in one bundle."

The exterior Self was peeling off, like his fleshly skin was—he was undergoing painful skin allergies which caused burning eruptions, blisters, rawness. But even as his old skin dried up and peeled off, he saw the tender new skin forming underneath.

Sometimes he woke up at early dawn in the hermitage and his childhood seemed to walk in the door. One morning he heard the tune, "The Whistler and His Dog." He hadn't heard it since he was five years old, when his father played the record on the phonograph. It made him realize his age. "I am now pushing fifty!" How could such a thing happen to someone like himself? "I am still too young to be thinking about 'old age,' really . . . I am the same person as the eighteen-year-old riding back alone into Bournemouth in a bus out of New Forest, where I had camped a couple of days and nights."

Yet he didn't look back at the past as something to analyze, but only to thank God for all he was and for all he was given to be. His past would never be simply a calendar leaf to tear off and throw away. Memory was not a loss but a gain, and he recalled how his Aunt Kit came once from New Zealand to visit him in the gatehouse. They sat drinking tea. It was the first time in forty years that he'd seen her, and they talked about memories, forebears, ancestors. She told

Tom his great-grandfather, James Merton, a bailiff, had come to New Zealand from Suffolk, England, with Tom's great-aunt. The bailiff's son, Charles, born in New Zealand, became a music teacher at Christ College, and his son Owen was Thomas Merton's father. Aunt Kit also shared memories of Gertrude Grierson, his grandmother, who died at age 102. Tom remembered how she had come to see them when he was very young and she taught him the Lord's Prayer. She had been born in Wales of a Scotch father.

"This is where our faces come from, the face Father had, that I have, that Aunt Kit has: the look, the grin, the brow. It is the Welsh in me that counts: that is what does strange things, and writes in the books, and drives me into the woods. Thank God for the Welsh in me. . . ."

One dawn, walking in the woods to pray the psalms, he watched the sun come up, rising like a great yolk of energy and spreading as if to take over the entire sky. He was struck with a vibrato-like sound. A sound too high for mortal ears, it was the wordless resonance of pure good. It filled all the spaces. The fields laughed and the forest seemed drunk and the very hills danced with joy. He understood.

"There is another kind of mercy than the mercy of Law which knows no absolution. There is a justice of newborn worlds which cannot be counted. There is a mercy of individual things that spring into being without reason. . . ."

Shantideva. "The unhappy are so because they have sought their own happiness; the happy are so because they have sought the happiness of others." *Shantideva* was a Buddhist word.

Father Louis Merton defined Shantideva as Franciscanism, and now that he was a hermit, he realized that "without this Franciscanism of Shantideva no religious solitude makes sense. What would be the use of being a hermit merely for self affirmation, even if one affirmed oneself in praise of God?"

Shantideva was to seek to be an instrument of God's peace, and this was where reality and visionary met, and it was where Buddhist monk and Catholic monk embraced.

Even though he was a hermit living in a hermitage, Merton had distinguished guests. In October of 1966, John Howard Griffin brought Jacques Maritain to see him. Maritain had come to Fort Worth to visit Griffin, his godson. They arrived in the autumn twilight at the gatehouse and there stood Merton, "dressed in his black and white monastic robes with a faded blue denim jacket and black woolen peacap."

To celebrate such guests, the dinner served them that night at the monastery consisted of soup, steak, vegetables, salad and dessert, with wine. Father Louis also partook of the meat, and "consumed it with enthusiasm," the guests noted.

The next morning, at Merton's hermitage in the wood, they sat in front of the fireplace. Merton built up a large fire of crackling logs to warm the old philosopher, Maritain, who sat in a rocking chair by the fire. Then Merton told his guests that he was doing a study on Bob Dylan and he played Dylan's revolutionary rock-ballads for the astonished old French philosopher. "Highway 61" resounded with its electric cadence through the primitive forest all around. Father Louis explained that the abbot let him have the phonograph and recordings for the research on his study of Bob Dylan, and that soon he would have to return them, when his article was completed.

Another distinguished visitor was Thich Nhat Hanh, a poet and a famous Vietnamese contemplative monk who was in the United States to take part in the peace movement. He had come to the monastery to pay his respects to a fellow contemplative who was equally a seeker after world peace. Father Louis and Nhat Hanh sang alleluias together at Gethsemani, and made a tape for their friend Daniel Berrigan in which Nhat Hanh sang a Buddhist gatha and Thomas Merton a Cistercian alleluia.

Thomas Merton wrote an essay, "Nhat Hanh Is My Brother":

"We are both monks . . . we have lived the monastic life about the same number of years. We are both poets, both existentialists. . . . It is vitally important that such bonds be admitted. They are the bonds of a new solidarity and a new brotherhood which is beginning . . . on all five continents . . . and cuts across political, religious, and cultural lines."

The alleluias Father Louis and Thich Nhat Hanh sang together that day were like a prelude to the Trappist monk's going forth into Asia to keep his appointment with the mystics of the East. An international Benedictine group, organized to help implement monastic renewal throughout the world, was sponsoring a conference of all Asian monastic leaders to be held at Bangkok, Thailand, in the middle of December 1968. Thomas Merton had been asked to deliver one of the principal addresses and his abbot had approved his acceptance of the invitation.

It was a warm August afternoon in 1968 when Brother Patrick Hart, a fellow Trappist, discussed with Merton the details of his forthcoming journey.

"As I approached the hermitage . . . I found Father walking slowly on a shady, well-beaten path at the edge of the woods overlooking the quiet valley, reading Dom Aelred Graham's new book on his Asian experiences. . . ."

Brother Patrick had been secretary to the former abbot, Dom James Fox, for nearly ten years, from 1957 to 1966. Much of Merton's writings had passed through his hands. For this reason the newly elected abbot assigned Brother Patrick as secretary to Father Louis Merton, to handle his correspondence and literary affairs while Merton was in Asia. Brother Patrick had just returned to Gethsemani from Rome, after two years away at the General's house in Rome, and he brought Father Louis a beautiful bronze cross, a gift from Pope Paul VI.

Now all was arranged. Everything was nearly ready for the Asian journey. When Dom Flavian Burns, the present abbot, discussed this pilgrimage with Father Louis, they both agreed that essentially it must be a journey to deepen his own experience of Asian wisdom and to bring this knowledge back to his monastery. As Merton himself put it, a few months later, in a mid-November talk he gave in Calcutta:

"I think we have now reached a stage, long overdue, of religious maturity at which it may be possible for someone to remain perfectly faithful to a Christian and Western monastic commitment and yet to learn in depth from, say, a Buddhist discipline and experience. I believe that some of us need to do this in order to improve the quality of our own monastic life and even to help in the task of monastic renewal."

But there was also another thing that Merton sought—a more solitary place. Visitors—hero-worshipers, seekers, friends —now continually besieged the abbey. There were intrusions, most of them innocent intrusions on the solitude of the holy man, but some were not so innocent. There were fanatics who came breathing fire and brimstone, promising to kill Thomas Merton. His writings on racial justice and peace were too strong, too influential. They were changing not only the Church but Western ways of thinking about Christianity, so that many people were perturbed. Merton received death threats, as all peacemakers have from the time of Christ, through Mahatma Gandhi and on to Martin Luther King, Jr.

But it was not fear of would-be snipers that made Father Louis and his abbot agree that he had to find a more solitary place. It was simply that Gethsemani had become a mecca, because the nation was going through more turmoil than the national psyche was able to bear. People came in search of some reassurance for the future.

On a day in early September, Father Louis celebrated his last Mass in the hermitage with Brother Patrick Hart and Brother Maurice and a few others. The candles glowed on the cedarwood altar and in the trees a thrush sang one long note. The passenger was ready and waiting.

Down the path from the hermitage they trooped, carrying boxes and bundles. Thomas Merton was wearing an odd combination of garments, including a beret and a Roman collar and jeans. In his bag he had a new washable suit, which Sister Gerarda washed during his stopover with the Trappistines at their monastery in the ancient redwood forest on the rugged northern California coast. He was considering it as a possible place for his solitary hermitage.

In San Francisco he got his Indonesian visa at the World Trade Center on the Embarcadero. Looking out over the bay, he prayed one of the Little Hours called Terce; then he was at the airport, enplaned, and being lifted skyward. The great wing was covered with rivers of cold sweat running backward and the window "wept jagged shining courses of tears"—good-by, America.

Gazing down he saw the earth's squares, triangles, rectangles, and thought: there Cain and Abel lay down red designs, and, he wondered, "Why had Cain suddenly become a hero in this day and age?" Was it just Herman Hesse's despair, or could Christ, the Lamb of God who takes away the sin of the world, save Cain?

When he first arrived in India, he was shocked to see how poor people really could be. "I went to put a small coin in the hands of a beggar and saw he was a leper whose fingers had been eaten away. . . . It's like that." Yet Calcutta had beauty—"the bizarre, macabre beauty of the disintegrating slums, the old fallen splendor . . . white cranes. . . ."

On the other wave-length of the spectrum was the rainbow-hued meeting with the Dalai Lama on the high mountain at Dharamsala, where he was taken by train from Delhi up the Himalayas.

He knew already how loved the Dalai Lama was by his people—"they are a beautiful, loving people. They surround his house with love and prayer. . . . Probably no leader in the world is so much loved by his followers and means so much to them."

On November 4, Father Louis wrote in his journal: "Today I am to see the Dalai Lama . . . but meanwhile the world goes on, and finance booms (zooms). We have run out of toilet paper and are using Saturday's newspaper. . . ." A few hours later he was having the audience. Despite his determination to stay with feet solidly on the ground, an intense brightness illuminated the encounter. It seemed the Dalai Lama, too, was determined not to be swept off his feet by the Trappist monk of such fame as a spiritual leader. He said he was glad to see Father Louis and had heard a lot about him. But within a few moments they were both deep in conversation about religion and philosophy and meditation, and before they knew it, hours had passed while they exchanged thoughts and confidences, talking about the methods of meditation, discipline, and spiritual knowledge. They were utterly open with each other like old friends and brothers.

By their third interview, the Dalai Lama was asking many questions about Western monastic life. Merton had said he hoped to bring back to his monastery something of Asian wisdom and the spiritual disciplines. The Dalai Lama told Merton that he, too, wished the same exchange, so that the monks of Buddhism could benefit from what was spiritually accessible in Christian monastic experience. Father Louis and the Dalai Lama felt a real spiritual bond. He called Merton a "Catholic geshe," which was the highest possible praise, a title of respect for a learned lama.

For Merton there was no barrier in his Judeo-Christian way-of-the-cross to the practice of the way-of-Zen.

"Zen is consciousness unstructured by particular form or particular system—it can shine through this or that system, religious or irreligious—as just glass—light shining through plain glass, no color—to regard Zen *merely* and *exclusively* as Zen Buddhism is to falsify it."

The Old Testament was part of the way, and when Father Louis was with the Dalai Lama, he thought about the visions of Ezekiel and the Apocalypse and wondered how the lamas would think of those visions. This unity within himself, to see truth on its many levels, included the Old Testament mystics, the New Testament mystics, and Zen and Buddhist mystics.

To Thomas Merton "the universe of the Old Testament" was "a praising universe . . . of which man is a living and essential part." He saw no spiritual well-being achieved by giving up one in order to obtain the other. Everything went together, just as, when one of the lamas composed a poem for Merton in Tibetan, Merton responded with a poem in English.

"In my contact with these new friends, I feel consolation in my own faith in Christ and His indwelling presence. I hope and believe He may be present in the hearts of all of us."

Chobgye Thiccen Rimpoche wrote a poem for Thomas Merton:

"To that beautiful one/Adored by all the Occident,/This bee wishes all the best/With its heartfelt delight."

And another *rimpoche* (Tibetan spiritual master), Chantral Rimpoche, cried in delight: "You are a rangjung Sangay, a natural Buddha!" Then, surprised at himself for getting on so well with one who had in no way abandoned his Christian nor even his Judeo past, he laughed and said: "There must be something wrong here!"

The *rimpoches* told him that seeking absolute solitude was wrong and showed lack of compassion. They were gently critical, too, of Christian religious wearing secular clothes. They tried to get Merton to wear his monk's habit, as all religious in India did. He tried, but only on formal occasions—otherwise he wore corduroy pants and a turtleneck jersey. The Tibetan monks found him faultless anyway.

"I have the feeling that everybody here knows all about everything and that as an 'American lama' I am a joyful and acceptable portent to all the Tibetans. Smiles everywhere."

To the love pouring out on him, Father Louis responded a thousandfold. He exhausted himself. He caught cold and could not throw it off. His body found the food hard to digest. "I am tired of too much food—and too much curry. Back to European food part of the time . . . I confess I am not very open to Hindu religion, as distinct from philosophy."

The Jesuits gave him throat lozenges, a Vicks inhaler, and double whiskeys. Nothing helped. And there were so many people everywhere!

"I am beginning to appreciate the hermitage at Gethsemani more than I did last summer when things seemed so noisy and crowded. Even here in the mountains there are few places where one does not run into someone. Roads and paths and trails are full of people. To have real solitude one would have to get very high up and far back!"

He decided that Alaska was probably the only place left where true solitude would be possible and exchanged letters with his abbot on the real possibility of founding a hermitage there.

"What do I care for a twenty-eight-thousand-foot postcard," he snorted at vast Kanchenjunga's snowy heights, "when I have this bloody cold?" Also, the coal smoke that filled the air of Dharamsala aggravated his bad throat.

"Today is Sunday at Gethsemani, half around the world

from here." He could see it as if he was back, that moment. Beyond the lofty white peaks of Kanchenjunga, just there, were the wooded hills of Nelson County, Kentucky, blue vineyard knobs with a scapular of mist on it.

The beggars had bled him dry of money. In Calcutta a woman followed him for three blocks sweetly murmuring: "Daddy, Daddy, I am very poor." He could only give her his last rupee, sad that it was not only all he had, but more than he could by now afford.

"But she is very poor. And I have come from the West, a Rich Daddy."

From the beginning of the Asian trip to the end, Thomas Merton remained the writer, noting down in his journal all the different impressions to remember: the cows on the steps of the hotel; students in saris raising money for flood relief; endless salaams; cafes where he was overcharged; beggars with arm stumps; old bathtubs—"old johns of the Raj. . . . Long life to the old johns of the Raj."

He realized he was trying to assimilate this exposure to Asia too quickly, and yet he knew Asia was not to be put in some category. "I do not get any impression of being called to come here and settle down." It was not his right place; yet the hermitage at Gethsemani was impossible also, because it was too turbulent. He could not forget the intrusions of last summer.

Other memories pulled his soul back—the deer in the woods that had been shot by hunters while he watched helplessly. The wounded animal had tried to escape; then bedded down, hiding, while hunters and dogs sought the dying beast. He, the monk, had hidden, like the deer, screened from the hunters. What could he do? Just pray. Suddenly hunters and dogs gave up. They went off. Then, incredibly, the deer leaped up and bounded away! A miracle.

Dreams haunted his nights and even his days. When he lay down for the afternoon siesta: "I was looking at the mountain and it was pure white, absolutely white. And I heard a voice saying—or got the clear idea of: 'There is another side to the mountain.' I realized that it was turned around and everything was lined up differently; I was seeing it from the Tibetan side."

He made a note to ask Sonam Kazi about dreams. Sonam Kazi was a lay Nyingmapa monk whom Merton had met while walking a mountain trail at Dharamsala. Sonam Kazi instructed Father Louis about mandalas.

Mandalas are mystical symbols for the universe. When correctly read by the initiate, they could induce liberating psychic and psychological knowledge, but, Merton felt, "this mandala business is, for me, at least, useless."

On December 5 he wrote: "My next stop will be the Bangkok meeting to which I do not especially look forward. . . . Certainly I am sick of the hotels and planes. But the journey is only begun. . . ."

December 10. At the morning session of the convocation of monks, a Jesuit priest, Father Jacques Amyot, talked on "The Monastery in the Human and Social Context of the Theravada Buddhist Countries of Southeast Asia."

After him, at 10 A.M., it was Thomas Merton's turn. His paper was entitled, "Marxism and Monastic Perspectives." Characteristically, Merton had chosen to speak to a spiritual convocation on the one subject which no one else would have tackled. Most others would have considered such a subject out of place among a group of spiritual holy monks.

Merton used the phrase "transformation of consciousness." The Marxist started with matter and moved up to a new structure "in which man will automatically develop a new consciousness." The traditional religions started "with the consciousness of the individual . . . to transform and liberate the truth in each person, with the idea that it will communicate itself to others." But the difference between the monk and the Marxist was fundamental, in that the Marxist was oriented to change of the economic structures, while "the monk is seeking to change man's consciousness."

Monastic preparation would lead eventually to the disappearance of structures, which were necessary, and yet were but scaffolding. They might be taken away—"and if everything is taken away, what do you do next? . . . Where do you go from the top of a thirty-foot pole?"

The large audience was buzzing excitedly when Thomas Merton's talk was finished. Where do you go from the top of a thirty-foot pole? A barrage of questions began. But the plan was to have all the questions saved up for the evening panel. Merton apologetically referred them to that evening session, saying: "So I will disappear."

The exhilarated mystics could practice the discipline of patience in the interim, and formulate more questions. Meanwhile, Merton and the other speakers at the conference went to lunch, and afterward to their respective rooms to rest.

Father Louis was tired. He was glad for the breeze of the whirring electric fan, and decided to take a shower. He took his shower and came out. Then? Somehow—no one really knows how—maybe he tried to turn the fan around or to move it closer to the bed—the fan fell on him and killed him.

Thomas Merton had received 220 volts of direct current into his body. The two Asian doctors who later examined him said his death was from heart failure due to the voltage of the fan. Yet others have survived 220 volts of electricity. Undoubtedly Merton's exhaustion and the cold he could not throw off had weakened his heart. Worst of all, he had been deprived of the element on which his life had come to depend—solitude. He was like one weakened by a long fast— he had had a feast of people, but a long fast of solitude.

Perhaps he could have been saved if those who heard his shouts had dared try his door, but they heard and went away out of respect for his privacy.

Merton shared the room with two other monks, who couldn't get in when they returned to the room two hours later. At last some abbots came and broke through the upper panel, opened the door, and went in. Thomas Merton was lying on his back, the fan on top of him. It was still going and had made a frightful burn on his chest. One of the abbots tried to remove the fan and himself received a severe electrical shock. Then someone had the presence of mind to run to the outlet and pull the cord from the socket.

The fan was damaged. Someone said the electric wiring was faulty, that it might have been tampered with. Someone else thought that the Central Intelligence Agency (CIA) could have got into the room and arranged the accident before Merton came back from lunch. The rumors are still flying around Asia.

During the Vietnam war Thailand was under tight security. The BKK CIA and the U.S. CIA worked closely together. Just a year or so earlier a secret paper was circulated by Bolivian General Hugo Banzer's government outlining strategy with CIA aid, against the Church. Archbishop Jorge Manrique Hurtado of La Paz was fingered, foreign priests and certain religious orders were named to be kept under surveillance, and the U.S. CIA "promised to provide full information on certain priests, especially those from the U.S.A." Bangkok was, at that time, a sinister city with uncontrolled vigilante groups whom idealistic peace-movement foreigners arriving from the United States would not even imagine existed. It was a most unsafe place for anyone with even a mild history in the anti-war movement, much less one who was famous as a priest with a strong influence toward pacifism. The U.S. CIA and the BKK CIA were provided with files on such priests from the moment they arrived. Yet, even if such were the facts, they would have been regarded as entirely irrelevant to himself by Thomas Merton. He had often said that God was using these things "to attain an end which I myself cannot at the moment see or comprehend"— and in the meantime—"that is His affair and not mine."

He had written in *No Man Is an Island*: "If, at the moment of our death, death comes to us as an unwelcome stranger, it will be because Christ also has always been to us an unwelcome stranger. For when death comes, Christ comes also, bringing us the everlasting life He bought for us by His own death."

Within a few hours after Father Louis Merton's body was found, the delegates to the Bangkok Conference wrote a heartbroken letter to Abbot Flavian Burns at Gethsemani:

"It was his presence here that drew us, and from the very moment of his arrival he was the center of all proceedings. . . ."

Twenty-seven years—to the day—after he entered the monastery, Thomas Merton died.

He had prophesied that he would disappear. He had prophesied that he would die the death of fire. "Those who die the death of fire—the death which Christianity was to call

martyrdom, and which Herakleitos definitely believed was a
witness to the Fire and the Logos . . . they live forever."

Who knows what he experienced in that electrical moment, he who had so often written his intimations of its
coming?

"All of a sudden . . . everything went crazy . . . inside
and outside your head began to explode. It was as if the universe was being thrown right at you. Then you came to and
you were living in the midst of these wires in a gray world
and everything had stopped. . . ."

He knew his dying. All his writings were his intimations of
his mortality, which was itself his intimation of immortality.

"On a dark night in the middle of the afternoon . . . I
dreamed I escaped from the hotel . . . where I was prisoned
. . . and there was nobody in the stairs to prevent my escape,
yet going down the stairs was like a lifetime. . . . Who is
waiting for me, behind the frosted glass doors. . . . Pray for
me, St. John of the Cross, to get through that door, where
the air comes under, where the light shines through, my
house being now at rest. On a dark night."

Two days before his death in Bangkok, Merton had writ-
ten Brother Patrick Hart: "I think of you all on this Feast
Day and with Christmas approaching I feel homesick for
Gethsemani. . . ."

He was home for Christmas. The body arrived at the
abbey early in the afternoon of December 17. His wish had
often been stated that he be buried in the cemetery at the
abbey, where the monks of Gethsemani had been buried for
the past 120 years. It was under these great cedars that he
had long meditated, that he had gone to sorrow for the death
of his younger brother, that he had gone to offer his joy over
the acceptance of his poems and his autobiography and all
his writings. There, at dusk, under a light snowfall his body
was laid beneath a solitary cedar tree, marked by a simple
white cross.

It is an old cemetery, old for America, and full of holy
ghosts.

FURTHER READING

Books by Thomas Merton

Seeds of Contemplation. New York: New Directions, 1949.

What Are These Wounds? New York: Bruce, 1950.

The Ascent to Truth. New York: Harcourt Brace Jovanovich, 1951.

Bread in the Wilderness. New York: New Directions, 1953.

The Last of the Fathers: Saint Bernard of Clairvaux and the Encyclical Letter. New York: Harcourt Brace Jovanovich, 1955.

The Living Bread. New York: Farrar, Straus & Giroux, 1956.

The Sign of Jonas. Garden City, N.Y.: Doubleday Image, 1956.

The Silent Life. New York: Farrar, Straus & Giroux, 1957.

The Secular Journal of Thomas Merton. New York: Farrar, Straus & Giroux, 1959.

Disputed Questions. New York: Farrar, Straus & Giroux, 1960.

Wisdom of the Desert. New York: New Directions, 1960.

The New Man. New York: Farrar, Straus & Giroux, 1961.

The Waters of Siloe. Garden City, N.Y.: Doubleday Image, 1962.

Life and Holiness. Garden City, N.Y.: Doubleday Image, 1964.

Seeds of Destruction. New York: Farrar, Straus & Giroux, 1964.

Gandhi on Non-Violence. (editor) New York: New Directions, 1965.

Seasons of Celebration. New York: Farrar, Straus & Giroux, 1965.

The Way of Chuang Tzu. New York: New Directions, 1965.

No Man Is an Island. Garden City, N.Y.: Doubleday Image, 1967.

Mystics and Zen Masters. New York: Farrar, Straus & Giroux, 1967.

Conjectures of a Guilty Bystander. Garden City, N.Y.: Doubleday Image, 1968.

Faith and Violence: Christian Teaching and Christian Practice. New York: Notre Dame, 1968.

Thoughts in Solitude. Garden City, N.Y.: Doubleday Image, 1968.

Zen and the Birds of Appetite. New York: New Directions, 1968.

My Argument With the Gestapo. Garden City, N.Y.: Doubleday & Company, 1969.

The Seven Storey Mountain. Garden City, N.Y.: Doubleday Image, 1970.

Contemplative Prayer. Garden City, N.Y.: Doubleday Image, 1971.

Thomas Merton on Peace. New York: McCall, 1971.

New Seeds of Contemplation. Rev. ed. New York: New Directions, 1972.

The Asian Journal of Thomas Merton. New York: New Directions, 1973.

Contemplation in a World of Action. Garden City, N.Y.: Doubleday Image, 1973.

A Thomas Merton Reader, edited by Thomas P. McDonnell, Garden City, N.Y.: Doubleday Image, 1974.

A Catch of Anti-Letters, by Thomas Merton and Robert Lax, Kansas City: Sheed, Andrews & McMeel, Inc., 1978.

The Monastic Journey. Garden City, N.Y.: Doubleday Image, 1978.

POETRY BY THOMAS MERTON

Thirty Poems. New York: New Directions, 1944.

A Man in the Divided Sea. New York: New Directions, 1946.

Figures for an Apocalypse. New York: New Directions, 1948.

The Tears of the Blind Lion. New York: New Directions, 1949.

The Strange Islands. New York: New Directions, 1957.

The Tower of Babel. New York: New Directions, 1957.

Selected Poems. New York: New Directions, 1959.

The Behavior of Titans. New York: New Directions, 1961.

Original Child Bomb. New York: New Directions, 1962.

Emblems of a Season of Fury. New York: New Directions, 1963.

Raids on the Unspeakable. New York: New Directions, 1966.

Selected Poems. Enlarged ed. New York: New Directions, 1967.

Cables to the Ace. New York: New Directions, 1968.

The Geography of Lograire. New York: New Directions, 1969.

BOOKS ABOUT THOMAS MERTON

Bailey, Raymond. *Thomas Merton on Mysticism.* Garden City, N.Y.: Doubleday Image, 1976.

Baker, James T. *Thomas Merton: Social Critic.* Lexington: University Press of Kentucky, 1971.

——. *Under the Sign of the Water-Bearer: A Life of Thomas Merton*. Louisville: Love Street Books, 1977.

Breit, M. *Thomas Merton: A Bibliography*. Metuchen, N.J.: The Scarecrow Press, 1974.

Chautard, J. B. *The Soul of the Apostolate* (Introduction by Thomas Merton). Garden City, N.Y.: Doubleday Image, 1961.

Dell'Isola, Frank. *Thomas Merton: A Bibliography*. Kent State University Press, 1975.

Finley, James. *Merton's Palace of Nowhere*. Ave Maria Press, 1978.

Griffin, John Howard. *A Hidden Wholeness: The Visual World of Thomas Merton*. Boston: Houghton Mifflin, 1970.

——. *Thomas Merton: Three Essays*. Thomas Merton Studies Center, Unicorn Press, 1969.

Hart, Bro. Patrick, ed. *Thomas Merton, Monk*. Garden City, N.Y.: Doubleday Image, 1976.

Higgins, John J. *Thomas Merton on Prayer*. Garden City, N.Y.: Doubleday Image, 1975.

Kelly, F. J. (S.J.) *Man Before God: Thomas Merton on Social Responsibility*. Garden City, N.Y.: Doubleday, 1974.

Labrie, Ross. *The Art of Thomas Merton*. Texas Christian, 1979.

Lentfoehr, Sr. Therese. *Words and Silences: On the Poetry of Thomas Merton*. New York: New Directions, 1979.

McInerny, D. Q. *Thomas Merton: The Man And His Work*. Cistercian Studies Series 27. Washington: Cistercian Publications, Consortium Press, 1974.

Nouwen, Henri J. *Pray to Live: The Contemplative Commitment of Thomas Merton*. Notre Dame, Ill.: Fides Publishers, 1972.

Palmer, Parker J. *In the Belly of a Paradox, the Thought of Thomas Merton*. Pendle Hill, 1979.

Rice, Edward. *The Man in the Sycamore Tree: The Good Times and Hard Life of Thomas Merton*. Garden City, N.Y.: Doubleday Image, 1972.

Twomey, Gerald, C.S.P. (Editor) *Thomas Merton: Prophet in the Belly of a Paradox.* New York: Paulist Press, 1978.

Voight, Robert J. *Thomas Merton: A Different Drummer.* Liguori, Mo.: Liguori Publishers, 1972.

Woodcock, George. *Thomas Merton: Monk—A Critical Study.* North Vancouver, British Columbia, Canada, Douglas & McIntyre, 1978.

INDEX

OTHER IMAGE BOOKS

OTHER IMAGE BOOKS

THE DEVIL YOU SAY! – Andrew M. Greeley

THE DIARY OF A COUNTRY PRIEST – Georges Bernanos

DIVORCE AND REMARRIAGE FOR CATHOLICS? – Stephen J. Kelleher

A DOCTOR AT CALVARY – Pierre Barbet, M.D.

EVERLASTING MAN – G. K. Chesterton

FIVE FOR SORROW, TEN FOR JOY – J. Neville Ward

THE FOUR GOSPELS: AN INTRODUCTION (2 vols.) – Bruce Vawter, C.M.

THE FREEDOM OF SEXUAL LOVE – Joseph and Lois Bird

THE FRIENDSHIP GAME – Andrew M. Greeley

THE GREATEST STORY EVER TOLD – Fulton Oursler

GUIDE TO CONTENTMENT – Fulton J. Sheen

GUILTY, O LORD – Bernard Basset, S.J.

HANS KÜNG: HIS WORK AND HIS WAY – Hermann Häring and Karl-Josef Kuschel

HAS SIN CHANGED? – Seán Fagan

HE LEADETH ME – Walter J. Ciszek, S.J., with Daniel Flaherty, S.J.

A HISTORY OF PHILOSOPHY: VOLUME 1 – GREECE AND ROME (2 Parts) – Frederick Copleston, S.J.

A HISTORY OF PHILOSOPHY: VOLUME 2 – MEDIAEVAL PHILOSOPHY (2 Parts) – Frederick Copleston, S.J. Part I – Augustine to Bonaventure. Part II – Albert the Great to Duns Scotus

A HISTORY OF PHILOSOPHY: VOLUME 3 – LATE MEDIAEVAL AND RENAISSANCE PHILOSOPHY (2 Parts) – Frederick Copleston, S.J. Part I – Ockham to the Speculative Mystics. Part II – The Revival of Platonism to Suárez

A HISTORY OF PHILOSOPHY: VOLUME 4 – MODERN PHILOSOPHY: Descartes to Leibniz – Frederick Copleston, S.J.

A HISTORY OF PHILOSOPHY: VOLUME 5 – MODERN PHILOSOPHY: The British Philosophers, Hobbes to Hume (2 Parts) – Frederick Copleston, S.J. Part I – Hobbes to Paley. Part II – Berkeley to Hume

A HISTORY OF PHILOSOPHY: VOLUME 6 – MODERN PHILOSOPHY (2 Parts) – Frederick Copleston, S.J. – The French Enlightenment to Kant

A HISTORY OF PHILOSOPHY: VOLUME 7 – MODERN PHILOSOPHY (2 Parts) – Frederick Copleston, S.J. Part I – Fichte to Hegel. Part II – Schopenhauer to Nietzsche

A HISTORY OF PHILOSOPHY: VOLUME 8 – MODERN PHILOSOPHY: Bentham to Russell (2 Parts) – Frederick Copleston, S.J. Part I – British Empiricism and the Idealist Movement in Great Britain. Part II – Idealism in America, the Pragmatist Movement, the Revolt against Idealism

OTHER IMAGE BOOKS

OTHER IMAGE BOOKS

OTHER IMAGE BOOKS

A 80 – 5